Dialogue with *Kelsey*

A Conversation with My Daughter
Before & After Her Death

Barbara Bennett

Legacy Book Press LLC
Camanche, Iowa

For Kelsey

"All goes onward and outward, nothing collapses,
And to die is different from what any one supposed, and luckier."

—Walt Whitman, "Song of Myself"

"It is only with the heart that one can see rightly; what is essential
is invisible to the eye."

—Antoine de Saint-Exupéry, *The Little Prince*

"Who would have thought my shrivel'd heart
Could have recover'd greennesse?

—George Herbert, "The Flower"

Table of Contents

Author's Note

A few hours after we learned our daughter had been killed in a bus-bicycle accident, I found an empty Moleskin notebook on my bedside table, tucked between a novel I was in the middle of reading and one I was planning to read. I'd kept the occasional diary over the years, but at that moment I felt an overpowering need to put my just-below-the-surface questions into words. I soon filled that notebook and, over the next three years, an additional five more. One afternoon, while on a walk near our Marrowstone Island home, I asked the universe—and more specifically my daughter—whether I could possibly do what at the moment seemed audacious: turn those notebooks into a memoir. Although I'd written a dissertation, edited a collection of essays, and published an academic article, I'd never written about my personal life with the intention of making it public. After reading an assortment of texts, gleaning whatever nuggets I could find about memoir-writing, I began. My first draft wasn't very good, but I signed up for classes, joined a writing group, attended workshops and retreats, sought editorial help, and added and deleted countless pages. Finally, after nine years, a memoir emerged that is close to what I envisioned.

Prologue

Mom, you need to stop thinking.

Since my daughter's death on June 1, 2012, I had longed to talk with her, to have a real back-and-forth conversation like we'd had throughout the twenty-eight years of her life. But I had to accept I'd never again hear the "Hi, Mom!" that always made me smile. A conversation between us was impossible. Wasn't it? But suddenly, there she was in my head, giving me advice!

Hi Mom! Do you remember the stories you read to us when I was growing up, the stories about enchanted places and magical creatures?

Of course, I remember them!

Well, those stories can help you now.

How is that, sweet girl?

You need to suspend the usual rules of time, place, and reason— just like in those stories.

I'll have to think about it.

No, Mom, that's the point, you need to stop thinking.

Kelsey was killed in a bicycle accident. I had imagined losing one of our three children—or at least I'd acknowledged the possibility. More than that was too awful to contemplate. And then it happened. Once the shock began to subside, I found myself endlessly asking, *Where is she?* I couldn't leave her alone in some unknown place. Absolutely not. I was her mother, and even though she was well into adulthood, I needed to be with her. I desperately wanted to talk with her, but what I ached for defied all reason and logic.

When our children were young, we had a bedtime ritual that lasted for a few years. I sat on Kelsey's bed, plaiting her long hair into a French braid while her younger brothers constructed Lego cities on the rug. When the braiding was done, I picked up a book from a nearby shelf and began reading aloud. Sometimes, if the book was a page-turner and we were close to the end, I read long past their bedtime. We made our way through chapter books like, *The Story of Doctor Dolittle; The Lion, the Witch, and the Wardrobe;* and scores of other titles. When the kids asked to read just one more chapter, I agreed—I didn't want the magic to end. Those were among the moments I missed most. But Kelsey was right. I needed to stop thinking. I began to pray, at odd intervals and then almost ceaselessly, *May I be open to what is beyond thinking, to what is hidden.*

Years ago, during a family vacation in France, we met a German man, a walking stick in one hand and a small pack on his back. A scallop shell was strung around his neck, identifying him as a pilgrim on the Camino de Santiago. He'd started his pilgrimage in Germany and, by walking a bit of the route each summer, he would finish, perhaps after many years, at the Cathedral of Santiago de Compostela in northern Spain.

Several years following Kelsey's death, I realized that I, too, have been on a pilgrimage, albeit an inner one. That journey began when Kelsey died and has led over the years, from a relationship as fragile as the wings of a butterfly to a connectedness that is part of every breath I take. Our conversation is sometimes with words, but often it's a vibration that soars above and resonates more deeply than spoken language, like jazz. It's a dialogue that softens my sorrow, holds me together, and opens me to the world beyond. My journey continues, ever changing, and I suspect it will for as long as I live.

chapter one
Moving

"You think I'm middle-aged?" I asked. Kelsey grinned and twisted her long hair into a knot.

"Hmm, yes, but just barely. According to our psychology class, middle age ends when you turn sixty-five."

"Okay. I have another year until I'm officially old."

The scent of lilacs drifted through the open windows, and sunlight warmed my back. Kelsey was interviewing me for her class on the psychology of women and needed to question someone in each age category. Apparently, I was the middle-aged representative. I really didn't care in what age group she placed me. I was just happy she was home.

I didn't consider myself much older than I was when our kids were young, but family photographs told a different story. In a photo taken soon after Kelsey's high school graduation, my graying hair contrasts with her lustrous brown curls. A picture taken at the time of her college graduation reveals the crevices of my neck, while her skin appears as smooth as a tide-washed stone. In a snapshot taken four years later at Seattle's Pike Place Market, our three kids are as vibrant as the surrounding marketplace, and my husband Craig and I fade into the background.

Because Craig was retiring on the first of June 2012, we had sold our Seattle house and bought another on an island off the Olympic Peninsula. We also leased a small apartment in Seattle to use until I retired the following June. In April, the kids returned to Seattle—Kelsey from Boston College where she was working toward her master's degree in Mental Health Counseling, Sam from the Master of Divinity program at Pacific School of Religion in Berkeley, and

Max from Swarthmore College outside of Philadelphia where he was an undergraduate—for a long weekend to sort through their belongings and say goodbye to their childhood home.

Sam and Max heaped their possessions into piles: what they wanted to save, what could go to a thrift store, what they were throwing away. Kelsey merely shifted her clothing, toys, and books from her drawers and bookshelves into cardboard boxes and, like a woodland mouse, saved everything. "Kelsey, you haven't gotten rid of a thing! Do you really want to keep high school newspapers and this ring from third grade? And what about this other stuff?" I asked, pointing to a pile of stuffed animals, miniature teacups, and childhood books.

"I love the ring, but I guess I don't want this anymore," she said, tossing a small doll into a discard box. "I can't decide which stuffed animals to get rid of so I'm keeping them all." I sighed. It was hard for Kelsey to leave anything—or anyone—behind.

The summer before we decided to move, I had offhandedly proposed to Craig, "Let's sell the house and retire to an island." He ran his fingers through what was left of his hair and grinned. "Okay with me," he replied. I was surprised. Ordinarily, Craig provided the counterbalance to my not-completely-thought-out suggestions. When Kelsey was old enough for kindergarten, I mentioned to him that we should check out private schools. Instead of giving me a definitive no, he announced that he was going to visit a nearby public school. I didn't want him to go without me, so a few days later we stood together on a public-school playground as bright-eyed five- and six-year-olds from a variety of ethnicities chased one another around the yard. A lump formed in my throat. Of course, we would enroll Kelsey in a public school.

When I wanted a new couch for our living room, Craig asked, "What's more important, furniture or a trip to Europe?" Europe won out, hands down. When I proposed taking the family to an expensive seafood restaurant to celebrate a special occasion, Craig offered to cook a multicourse dinner at home. Yet when I suggested moving to an island in the Salish Sea, he had no objections.

We searched real estate listings and visited properties on various islands near Seattle until, eventually, a clear vision of what I was looking for formed in my mind: a house in a sunlit clearing, surrounded by forest. When Kelsey was home for Christmas, we took her to look at a house on Whidbey Island—a short drive and a ferry ride from Seattle. "I know Dad could be happy here, sitting and reading for most of the day, but what about you, Mom?" she asked after touring the house. "Wouldn't you miss your book clubs and your friends?"

"I'd find a coffee shop and talk with my *new* friends. And I'd walk the dog," I replied.

She smiled. "I guess you're planning on getting a dog." We didn't have a dog at the time, but apparently my vision of our future home included one. Even though the Whidbey Island house was charming, I kept squinting, trying to see the land around the house from a different perspective. But no matter how I focused my gaze, it didn't fit my mental image of a sunlit clearing in the woods.

In February, we learned of a house for sale on Marrowstone Island. Since we knew nothing about Marrowstone, we did some research and discovered that the island is barely seven miles long and only a quarter mile wide at its narrowest point. On a map, Marrowstone and its sister island, Indian Island, jut out from the Olympic Peninsula like the crusher and pincer claws of a crab.

We caught a ferry from Seattle to Bainbridge Island and stood on the deck for a few minutes, breathing in the cold salt air before retreating to the shelter of the cabin. After leaving Bainbridge and crossing the Hood Canal, we traveled along the gray-blue Salish Sea, waves rippling in the wind, low clouds like a strand of pearls poised above the distant shore. A graceful bridge spanning a narrow expanse of water led to Indian Island, which is home to the West Coast's largest US Naval magazine with an underground weapons repository. The road passed between a county park on one side and a barbed wire fence on the other. I tried to ignore the deadly arsenal buried beyond the barbed wire, but my shoulders tensed until we crossed the causeway dividing the two islands and saw a sign about the next meeting of the Marrowstone Island Community Association.

Dazzled by views of sparkling bays, snowcapped mountains, and verdant pastures that sloped to the sea, we meandered along island roads until coming to Mystery Bay—so named because its entrance is hard to discern from the sea—and to the tiny town of Nordland on the banks of the bay: three or four houses, a pocket-sized post office, and the Nordland General Store. A couple of Adirondack chairs on the porch of the store stood next to a large, Styrofoam cooler filled with fresh oysters. Inside, by the hot dog buns and condiments, a wood-burning stove churned out enough heat to counter the brisk February weather outside. "Do you live on the island?" I asked a man as he poured coffee from the pot on top of the stove.

"Yep," he said, taking a sip from his steaming mug, "just down the road."

"What's it like to live here?"

"It's a good place, a real community."

On the side of the store, next to a parking lot large enough for two cars, a huge sign in white letters on a blue background, proclaimed:

"Marrowstone, a Small Island Slightly off the Coast of North America, where all the people are friendly, and all the beaches are clothing optional."

The "For Sale" sign on East Marrowstone Road led us up a winding dirt driveway. Native blackberry vines sprawled beneath salmonberry bushes; grand cedars soared above rhododendrons; and flattened sedges were indications of a deer sanctuary. As we drove under low branches that brushed against the top of our car, we caught fleeting glimpses of the house: tall, gray, with a dark-red door. Once we emerged into the clearing, I stared at the house, amazed. Set in a sunlit glade and surrounded by forest, it was exactly what I had imagined—and what I'd been looking for throughout the past months. We made an offer that day and moved in on the first of May 2012.

chapter two
The Unspeakable

It was June 2, 2012. Early morning sunlight filtered through the clouds, beginning to illuminate the sparse furnishings in our recently-leased Seattle apartment. Two boxes of books, still unopened, rested next to an empty bookcase. I had just finished cooking Chicken Marsala to share with friends we'd invited for a weekend on Marrowstone. Once the chicken and makings for a salad were packed into a cooler by the door, I sat on the couch and watched the sun rise over the Cascade Mountains.

My ninety-year-old father had died three weeks before. We weren't expecting him to live much longer than his nine decades, but his death left me feeling surprisingly exhausted and unmoored. Mom and Dad had lived with us for eight years until Dad became so incapacitated by Parkinson's disease that we could no longer care for him in our home. For the past year, he had been living in the skilled nursing unit of a Christian retirement center, and Mom was around the corner in one of the center's independent apartments.

The first time Dad saw his room in the retirement center, I was nervous, wondering what he would think about living in a nursing facility and how he would feel about not sharing a bed with Mom for the first time in almost seventy years. He looked around, trying to get his bearings. His toiletries were on top of the dresser, a familiar and beloved blanket covered the bed, and a riot of pink rhododendrons was blooming outside the sliding glass doors. A nurse poked her head into the room, and Dad asked her, "How long will I be here?"

"Until Jesus calls you home," she answered cheerfully.

Relief flooded my body when Dad responded with laughter. *He'll be okay,* I thought.

Dad died eleven months later during his afternoon nap. I'd been with him in the morning and had just returned to work when I got the call and hurried back. Mom was sitting next to his bed, stroking his hand. "I didn't think this would happen now," she whispered.

"I didn't either," I replied. I'd thought we would have some kind of warning. Even though Dad had been more confused than usual, unable to eat lunch without my help, I assumed he only needed to have his medications adjusted. As it turned out, his confusion *was* our warning, but I'd missed it.

The day before he died, as Mom brushed Dad's hair and buttoned his sweater, he said to her softly, "You're so beautiful." She was startled. Dad rarely said anything other than "yes," "no," and "I love you." After his death, Mom repeated his comment—to me, to my brothers, and to the friends and family members who called to express their condolences. Those heartfelt words were Dad's last gift to her.

That June morning as we left Seattle on our way to Marrowstone, the weather was cold and misty, typical for late spring in the Pacific Northwest. We were driving along Highway 104, having headed out of the small coastal town of Kingston, when my cell phone rang. "This is the Boston police," a brusque male voice said. "Are you related to Kelsey Rennebohm?" My stomach clenched. *What's wrong?* I thought. *Has Kelsey been robbed? Has she lost her phone?*

"Yes, I'm her mother. Is she okay?"

Ignoring my question, he stated briskly, "I have to verify some things. Are you driving right now?"

"Yes." I willed him to reassure me, to tell me that Kelsey was okay. Anything else was unthinkable. Craig, listening to my part of the conversation, pulled the car into a Chevron station, fifteen or so yards from the gas pumps and next to a tangled hedge of blackberry vines. I answered questions about Kelsey's birth date, address, and phone number, still hoping that the problem had to do with a minor incident. The officer said, "Your daughter was in a bicycle accident."

No!

"And was hit by a bus last night."

No, no!

"Unfortunately, she was killed."

I tried to connect his first word with the last. *Unfortunately* meant getting stitches or suffering from a concussion, not *killed.* I threw the phone on the seat, thrust open the front passenger door, and fell on my knees in the gravel, unable to catch my breath, feeling as though I'd been pounded by a crushing wave. I looked at a man in the distance who was walking in slow motion from his car to a gas pump—and then everything went dark. I don't know how long I stayed there, probably not long, but when I pushed myself up, off the ground, my life had changed forever.

chapter three
Sally

His face pale and drawn, his shoulders slumped, Craig suddenly looked decades older. We sat in the car, not touching, not crying, not saying a word until after what seemed like eternity, he asked me how we should get home. I tried to weigh the choices—two possible ferry routes or avoiding ferries altogether by driving around the Sound—but I couldn't get my shattered brain to function. "Let's go back the way we came."

As Craig turned the car around, I started making phone calls, the first to Sam, who said he'd be waiting for us at our apartment—he had just completed his master's program and was staying with us until he and his girlfriend, Annie, could find a place of their own. Sam offered to call Max at his college outside of Philadelphia. I phoned my brothers, Craig's sisters, and a few friends—probably seven or eight calls in all—telling each person who answered only what the Boston police officer had told me and then hanging up without saying goodbye. I didn't want to hear their responses. I sensed that a word—or a touch—could turn me to sand. Stillness seemed the safest place. I placed the phone on my lap and stared at the road, unable to link my thoughts coherently.

All of a sudden, memories from the day my sister, Sally, died—February 17, 1958—rose from the debris of my muddled brain. It seemed like no time had intervened between then and the present, awful moment.

My family—Mom, Dad, my younger sister, two brothers, and my maternal grandfather—lived in a pre-World War II bungalow in a central Illinois university town. I was nine, Sally had just turned seven, and my brothers John and Jim were five and three.

"I don't feel good," I whispered. Mom glanced at me, her eyes soft with concern, and nodded.

"Then I think you better stay home," she said gently.

I lowered my spoon next to the bowl of uneaten cereal, wandered slowly into the living room, and made a nest on the couch. I tried to make sense of what I had just learned from Mom: Sally was in a coma, and although I wasn't sure what that meant, I knew it wasn't good. After what seemed like hours, Mom and Dad asked me to accompany them upstairs. As we sat on the top step with me wedged between Mom's soft wool skirt and Dad's scratchy trousers, I focused on my feet, afraid of what I might see if I looked at either of them, until Dad tapped my shoulder.

"You know Sally's been sick," he said. I nodded. My sister had been sick for the past two years. I'd grown accustomed to her constant fatigue and occasional hospitalizations for blood transfusions. Often, she was too exhausted to do anything other than lie in bed, drawing pictures and looking through the books she was learning to read in her first-grade classroom—when she was well enough to be in school. My parents didn't tell us the underlying reason for Sally's hospitalizations and unrelenting fatigue. They thought it would be best for us four kids to live life as normally as possible—but I knew our lives, especially Sally's, weren't normal.

As we sat together on the stair, Dad cleared his throat and said quietly, "Sally has leukemia." I must have looked confused because he added, "Do you remember Red Skelton's little boy?" I nodded. Red Skelton was a comedian I'd often seen on TV. I had read a magazine article about his nine-year-old son's illness and recent death.

"Sally has leukemia, like Red Skelton's boy," Dad explained.

I inhaled sharply. "Is *Sally* going to die?"

"Yes."

When I remember that moment, it's as though I'm watching the three of us in a slow motion, silent film, but probably it was only a few seconds until I managed to ask, "When?"

"We don't know for sure," Dad replied. "That's up to God. But the doctor thinks it'll be soon."

The three of us stayed there, pressed against one another, until Dad and Mom grimly made their way back to Sally's bedroom, and I wrapped myself in a protective layer of silence on the living room couch. My younger brothers—crumpled cowboy hats over their ears and toy holsters around their small hips—had gone to a neighbor's house. My grandpa, a widower who had moved in with us six years before, was reading, his back slumped and his head sagging like trampled blades of grass. Sometime in the afternoon, my paternal grandparents arrived from their farm town forty miles away. After taking off their galoshes and hanging their heavy coats in the hall closet, they joined us in the living room. My grandma, her face somber, sat down on the couch next to me and patted my back but said nothing. My grandpa adjusted his glasses and eased into a nearby chair. The three of them might have talked among themselves, but I wasn't paying attention. Instead, I tried to remain as still as possible in a world that threatened to spin out of control.

Around dusk, my grandma pulled the curtains across the front window and turned on the lamps. A little while later, Dad, his eyes red, came into the living room. "Sally's in heaven with Jesus," he said. I remember hearing muffled sobs and someone clearing his or her throat, but what I remember most distinctly is that at long last I could breathe. I'd been holding my breath throughout the entire day—and perhaps throughout the previous two years. *It's over,* I thought.

Throughout her illness, Sally had gotten special attention. Dad took her on outings to the park and on overnight trips to my grandparents' home. The Easter before Sally died, a man-sized white bunny knocked on our door and handed me a huge basket filled with candy and toys. "This is for Sally," the bunny said. My heart sank. *Not for me,* I thought. I knew Sally got a lot of attention because of her illness, but I believed that was also because she was sweet and lovable, whereas I was often resentful and not nearly so adorable.

Much later, when I was twenty-seven or twenty-eight and getting a massage from an intuitive practitioner, with soft music playing in the background, I suddenly began to weep. And a question that had hovered just below my awareness for years, finally asserted itself: *Did Mom and Dad wish it had been me who died rather than Sally?*

A few minutes after hearing of Sally's death, I made my way down the hall to the bathroom and stopped at the open door. Dad was sitting on the closed toilet seat, his head bowed, his hands covering his head, shaking with sobs that sounded like a thundering storm. I've never forgotten that sound nor the sight of my dad so completely undone.

The small casket at Sally's funeral in our Presbyterian church was surrounded by mounds of flowers. Seated next to my parents in the front pew —and overpowered by the sickly-sweet scent of the flowers—I found it difficult to concentrate on the service. At some point, we were invited to view the open coffin. Sally was in her best navy-blue dress with its lacy collar, her favorite toy—a small stuffed cat—next to her. Her formerly straight, light brown hair had become dark and wavy, and her face was puffy because of the heavy steroids she'd been taking. Despite these illness-related alterations—she looked a lot like me. This rattled me. I worried that I, too, might get sick and die.

The first Easter after Sally's death, my parents, brothers, and I planted a peony bush next to her gravestone and set a basket filled with brightly colored eggs beside it. On Memorial Day, we brought bouquets of handpicked flowers to her grave; on the Fourth of July, tiny flags; and on Christmas, a small tree, decorated with homemade ornaments. I talked with Sally before falling asleep each night, telling her about my day and how much I missed her. I imagined the two of us walking home from school, my dress brushing against hers, our hands almost touching.

When I couldn't sleep because I feared dying, Dad tried to re-assure me. "Remember the story of Henny Penny?" he asked one night. "How she ran around, scared that the sky would fall? We have to keep on living, not being afraid of what might happen. The sky didn't fall on Henny Penny, and it won't fall on you." I was com-forted by my father's words at the time, but when we got the phone call from the Boston police telling me of Kelsey's death, I knew that the sky had fallen.

chapter four
Ocean of Light

"Aunt Barb, Uncle Craig," our nephew Benj murmured as Craig and I staggered into our Seattle apartment, barely able to put one foot in front of the other. Lithe and with spiky ginger-colored hair, he looked younger than his forty years. I remembered him as a sweet five-year-old, a gangly teenager, and a college art major whose art installations pushed past the norm. He positioned an open folding chair next to the couch and pulled another from the stack on the floor. I realized, with the part of my brain that could still focus, that he and Sam were setting up chairs for family members and friends. I hadn't considered that others would want to be with Craig, Sam, and me. Sam glanced up at us, his face pallid beneath his short dark beard. Although I'd rebuffed a hug from Craig's sister in the lobby of our apartment building—the thought of touching anyone unbearable to me—I wrapped my arms around my eldest son's six-foot-two frame, centering my attention on his breath, on the warmth of his body, and on the strong beating of his heart. This beloved child of ours was still alive.

Only twenty months younger than Kelsey, Sam had shared so much with her: the back seat of a double stroller, the same preschool, elementary school, high school, and university. For a short while, they even shared an apartment in Harlem. Sam rented the apartment at the beginning of his sophomore year at Columbia University, and, when Kelsey unexpectedly found herself in the city without a home, let her move in until she could find her own place. Kelsey's bags and boxes took up most of the bedroom floor, but what really irritated Sam was her expectation that the two of them would talk over the events of each day—like she always had done with her roommates in college. According to Kelsey, their nightly conversation went something like this:

"How was your day, Sam?" she'd ask.

"Fine."

"Well, what happened? Anything special?"

"No, just a regular day."

"Come on, Sam. Can't we talk about what's going on in our lives?

"Kelsey, it was just a regular day. What more do you want me to say?"

Kelsey was hurt, and Sam was frustrated. Even though she eventually found her own apartment, Kelsey never stopped pushing Sam to talk about his feelings. And Sam never stopped resisting. I was afraid that the memory of their disagreements would make his grief more complicated, but on that day, just hours after learning of Kelsey's death, there was no way I could put my uneasiness into words. I remembered how neglected I had felt during Sally's illness and how anxious I'd been after her death. I wanted Sam and Max to know that, with every fiber of my being, I adored them, to know that I was grateful beyond words *they* were still alive. I tried to show this by helping Sam with the chairs, but unfolding even one left me drained. I rested my hand on his arm for a moment and then retreated to Craig's and my bedroom.

As afternoon sunlight filtered through the blinds, I tugged the bedcovers up to my neck and closed my eyes. A cataclysmic storm threatened my body, so I lay as still as possible, fearing to move even an inch. A soft murmur of voices from the living room rose and fell like gentle waves with occasional surges of soft laughter. *How can anyone laugh?* I wondered. Then another memory, from two years before, came to mind: I was visiting Kelsey in New York where she was, at the time, teaching school. Her best friend and apartment mate, Katie, had just come into the bedroom, tossing back her brunette hair, her brown eyes twinkling with amusement,. "Well, that was officially one of the worst dates I've ever had," she announced as she flung herself onto the bed next to Kelsey and me.

"So, dating someone from Jdate wasn't what you'd hoped it would be?" Kelsey asked with a smile.

Katie chuckled and shook her head. "It was worth a try. I thought maybe a random Jewish guy would be better than a random Christian guy. Anyway, it was awful. When he started talking about some team, I told him I wasn't all that into sports. He didn't get it."

Kelsey's giggles were like water bubbling over rocks. Between bouts of laughter, she asked, "He really didn't talk about anything else?"

"No! I kept trying to bring up other subjects. But this is what made it so much worse: he talked while he was eating. Food kept dribbling out of the corners of his mouth."

By then both young women were clutching their sides, convulsed with laughter. When she finally could talk, Kelsey gasped, "So I guess you won't be going on a second date," setting off another spasm of laughter.

Kelsey won't ever laugh again, I thought, as the memory receded. *Can I no longer think of her laughter without pain?* I felt a flash of rage at the injustice of the notion but pulled up the quilt until it covered my head and tried to block all further memories.

Late in the afternoon, after the initial shock subsided, a tsunami of pain flooded my body, and I began to cry—sobs that turned into high-pitched wails and then into a kind of keening that shook my entire body. My mother, sisters-in-law, and dear friend Lise—who, along with her husband, had planned to spend the weekend with Craig and me on Marrowstone—heard me and rushed into the bedroom to caress my face, support my head, and rub my back. They murmured soft phrases that felt like an embrace. I don't know how long they stayed with me, but at some point, I collapsed into a troubled sleep.

I awoke alone a while later and sat up, staring at something in the corner of the room: a swirling fog that made the hair rise on the back of my neck. There was a power around me that was stronger and more absolute than anything I had ever experienced—and it aroused in me a terrifying sense of awe. Abraham must have felt this when he was told by God to sacrifice his beloved son Isaac. Although I never left the bed, I felt like I had dropped to my knees.

Then all at once, the air in the room became less oppressive, less frightening. I took a deep breath. Something caught my eye, and I turned my head toward the wall behind the bed. Above the spindles of the cherry headboard, I could make out hazy forms: tiny yellow sparks that twirled and leaped with joy like the Matisse cutouts that Kelsey had fallen in love with years before on a family trip to Paris.

I stared in confusion. *What is this?* I wondered. It bewildered me. *How can there be ecstasy amid sorrow and pain?*

Craig came into the room. I reached for his hand—my strength seemed to come from the point where our hands connected—and turned to look at the wall behind the bed. The dancing figures, visible only to me, were still there, although they were becoming hazier. Certain that he knew the right words, I asked Craig, "Tell me something about how this pain might one day change."

He closed his eyes and said quietly, "Nothing is ultimately lost but is gathered into God's infinite care and returned to us as possibility." It was a paraphrase from Alfred North Whitehead, the late nineteenth and early twentieth-century mathematician and philosopher.

A few years later, a Quaker friend read me a quotation from the journals of George Fox, the English mystic who founded Quakerism in the seventeenth century: "I saw, also, that there was an ocean of darkness and death, but an infinite ocean of light and love, which flowed over the ocean of darkness. And in that also I saw the infinite love of God; and I had great openings."

My vision was similar to George Fox's. On that afternoon of darkness and death, I was given an opening, a glimmer of light. Although I didn't know how I'd get there or how long it would take, there was the *possibility* that once again I would experience joy.

chapter five
Kelsey's Bike

As that long and painful afternoon of anguish turned into evening, recollections—often just fragments—flashed through my head, like electricity arcing from one part of my brain to another: the red-and-white polka-dotted dress Kelsey fell in love with when she was four and wore for every special occasion; the multiple rings she placed on each finger—one sporting a troll with bristly orange hair—and wore continuously throughout the second and third grades; the mobile she carefully put together in fifth grade to illustrate Anne Frank's diary; the purple bridesmaid dress she had worn in the recent wedding of a childhood friend. And her bike.

Kelsey found her bike at Brooklyn Flea, the borough's renowned flea market, although she had dreamed of becoming an urban biker long before then. Tired of crowded subways, she craved a different kind of experience—less stifling, more sensual—on her commutes to work: the touch of a breeze, the voices of children playing, the buttery scent of *pan dulce* baking in a nearby *pandería*. The last time I'd visited her in New York, Kelsey wanted to show me where she'd gotten her bike. Because the flea market didn't open until mid-morning, we went out for breakfast at a nearby bistro. Although we stood in line for nearly an hour before being seated, I didn't mind. I couldn't think of a better way to spend a Saturday morning than having breakfast in Brooklyn with Kelsey.

Afterward, we walked along a broad path in Prospect Park beneath brilliant red and yellow leaves as cyclist after cyclist zipped past us. Along the way, we saw one of Kelsey's former boyfriends. He braked his bike and stood, talking with us, for a few minutes before resuming his ride. While they were dating, he had encouraged her to get her own bike, also mentioning Brooklyn Flea as a good place to find one.

Kelsey and I climbed the steep steps to the playground of PS #321—which on weekends transformed into the flea market—and were immediately confronted with row after row of used bicycles, some of them with torn seats, most with dented rims, and all of them littermates to her own mutt of a bike. "Here it is, Mom," Kelsey said. "Here's where I found my bike. Every week this section seems to get bigger. It's just so cool!"

I nodded, appreciating her enthusiasm but not feeling the same pull toward bicycles. "Yep, there certainly are a lot of them," I said, giving the bikes a cursory glance and turning my attention to the nearby tables covered with dishes, tablecloths, and assorted cooking items. "How about browsing other sections?" Kelsey nodded, reluctantly moving away from her favorite part of the market.

After purchasing her bike and riding around her neighborhood for a few weeks, she became confident enough to cycle into Manhattan, eventually making it all the way to the East Harlem school where she taught mostly Black and Brown middle schoolers. She'd been hired to teach Spanish, but the job was contingent on her also being willing to teach one PE class. Although she was fluent in Spanish, she'd never played a sport other than during her last semester in high school, when she and several other girls formed a rugby team and Kelsey was the hooker. In lieu of trying to teach soccer, which she knew little about, she asked her students to demonstrate the skills needed for the game and ended each class with a ten-minute reflection on what had gone well and what had not. Her students loved Kelsey's approach. At the end-of-the-year assembly, many of the middle schoolers said that Kelsey was their favorite PE teacher. "Can you imagine, Mom?" she exclaimed. "Me, their favorite PE teacher!"

Kelsey's commute to Harlem required navigating Brooklyn streets for seven miles, crossing the Brooklyn Bridge, and riding another nine miles up the East River Greenway. When she moved to Brookline, a suburb of Boston, for graduate school after nine years of living in New York, Kelsey was determined to continue biking. Max took the bus from his college in Pennsylvania to help her with the move. Once they'd finished unloading all the boxes, he rented a bike from a neighborhood bicycle shop, and the two of them rode into and around Boston. That night, Kelsey called me. "Boston seems like much more of a town than a city," she said. I sighed, relieved that she had exchanged the dangers of biking through New York City for the seemingly safer streets of Boston. But, as I later learned, New York City—with its multiple bike paths—was far safer for cyclists than Boston.

Was the accident my fault? The question tormented me. *I should have forbidden her to ride,* I thought. Never mind that, at twenty-eight, she'd been an adult for the past ten years and would have scoffed at the suggestion. I worried that I might have missed something vital. *Did I fail to make sure she was strong, agile, and careful enough to be an urban biker?* Although I told her I was worried about her biking—especially in New York City—she reassured me by saying that she was a defensive rider, always checking for open car doors, and that she traveled along bike paths as much as possible. But the most important task of a mother is keeping her child safe, and I had failed.

Was the accident Kelsey's fault? The question twisted in my brain like a corkscrew. *Had she been reckless?* I reflected on a moment when she was about seven months old—adept at crawling and determined to investigate every corner of the house. One day, after playing with assorted bowls and spoons in the kitchen, she crawled to where the kitchen linoleum met the dining room carpet and carefully turned around to back over the raised threshold. Her father watched with an amused smile. "Did you see how cautiously she navigated that slight rise?" We laughed, but I never forgot the moment—it seemed to reveal something intrinsic to our daughter.

The same guardedness continued throughout Kelsey's elementary and middle school years. She was a bit of a homebody. Although she enjoyed the first few hours of a sleepover with neighborhood friends, at around ten o'clock she would start to cough and a few minutes later announce, "I think I'm getting sick. I need to go home."

When she became old enough to drive, Kelsey shed a layer or two of circumspection. The morning of her fifteenth birthday, she declared that she was eligible for her learner permit and asked me to give her a ride across town to the Department of Motor Vehicles. She was rarely that adamant, so I rearranged my schedule and picked her up the minute school let out. We stood in line for hours at the DMV, but once Kelsey had her permit in hand, she flashed me a huge grin, the long wait completely forgotten.

After hours of circling the empty parking lot of a nearby middle school, learning how to shift gears of our old Volvo station wagon, she was ready to drive around our Seattle neighborhood. I practiced deep breathing as I tried to coach her along the narrow, hilly streets, but after a few white-knuckle lessons I could no longer tolerate the anxiety and turned the instruction over to Craig. Hoping to awaken her inner monk, he attempted a Zen-like approach. "Feel the road, feel the wheel," he said, with great emphasis, as they began their first session. (When they returned home, Kelsey performed a fond but wicked imitation of her dad's method of teaching.)

One Saturday morning, we headed to a large shopping center in the University District with Kelsey behind the wheel, me in the passenger seat, and Sam in the seat behind us. Kelsey had never parked in a busy lot, and although the thought of her doing so made me apprehensive, I figured I could talk her through it. "There's a parking spot!" I said, pointing to an empty space between two parked cars. I was ready to tell her the next step when she abruptly rotated the steering wheel ninety degrees and zipped into the space, luckily missing the adjacent cars by mere inches. "Way to go, Kelsey!" Sam shouted, clearly impressed by this new and more daring side of his sister. When, finally, I could breathe again, I said in a distinctly un-Zen-like voice, "For God's sake, Kelsey, use the brakes!" She nodded but later asked her older cousin Kira to take over the instruction.

Kelsey's zeal for driving was a harbinger of her later fervor for more daring adventures. She chose to attend college in New York, one of the most diverse and exciting cities in the world; spent part of her junior year in Quito, Ecuador where she became friends with members of an indigenous community who were reclaiming their land rights by squatting on a city-owned hill; and returned the following summer to live in their community, teaching English to the children and conducting interviews for her senior thesis. Toward the end of that summer, Sam met her in Quito, and they traveled throughout Ecuador, Bolivia, and Peru. The following year, she counseled youth in the Dominican Republic and returned to New York to take a job in the South Bronx, one of the poorest neighborhoods of the city.

I realized that my sometimes-wary baby had become very bold—not reckless, but willing to take risks to explore the world and to help people improve their lives. *Had she taken a risk that led to her death?* I didn't know the answer to that question.

chapter six

Dreams and Memories

Four days before her death, Kelsey told me about a dream she'd had the night before: *I was in a bus with all the family—you, Dad, Sam, Max, all my aunts, uncles, and cousins… Everyone. I was getting close to my stop, and I had this feeling of dread. Then I got off the bus and started crying. I felt so sad.*

When I remembered the dream on the drive back to Seattle after the phone call from the Boston police, a shiver went down my spine. *Had her death been planned? Did she know, on some level, that she would die soon?* I'd never held with the view that our lives are pre-planned, but perhaps, through some kind of time warp, one can have an unconscious awareness of approaching death. Since I'd gotten the news of Kelsey's death, anything seemed possible.

After she recounted the dream, I responded by saying, "Seems like you've been on a journey since Papa B died."

"Yeah, I guess so," Kelsey acknowledged. "It's been hard since I got back. I keep thinking of all of you and missing you."

Dad's extended family had gathered for his memorial service in the large fellowship hall of Mom and Dad's retirement center. Even when Dad could no longer carry on a conversation due to Parkinson's-related dementia, his eyes lit up whenever he saw family members or friends, and he still said, "I love you," to Mom and to his children, grandchildren, nieces, and nephews, all of whom were present for his memorial service on May 20, 2012—just twelve days before Kelsey's fatal accident.

Before his memory and cognition began to falter, Dad loved to talk about Jesus and, with almost as much fervor, the Chicago Cubs. He was also extremely fond of donuts. He frequently took his grandkids to his favorite donut shop and always struck up a conversation with the salesclerk and anyone else who happened to be there. His grandkids said they could count on going out for donuts with their Papa B and making at least one new friend along the way.

At the service, we sang the old hymns, "How Great Thou Art" and "Softly and Tenderly Jesus Is Calling," concluding with Steve Goodman's funny ode to the Chicago Cubs, "A Dying Cub Fan's Last Request." Wrigley Field, the home of the Chicago Cubs, was sacred to Dad. When our kids and their cousins were young, we took an extended family trip to the Midwest, including, of course, a visit to Wrigley Field. Each year at the end of the regular baseball season, when it became clear the Cubs weren't going to be in the World Series or even come close to being in the playoffs, Dad would pump his fist in the air and declare, "We'll get it next year!" In the fall of 2016, when the Cubs won the World Series for the first time since 1908, the victory was bittersweet. After more than eight decades of being a devoted fan, Dad wasn't alive to share the celebration.

A year or so after his death, both of my brothers and two of my nephews visited Wrigley Field with small packets containing Dad's ashes tucked into their pockets. They asked a security guard, "What would happen if someone tried to scatter ashes on the field?"

"Well," replied the guard with a slight smile, "if anyone saw them do it, they'd be told to stop."

My brothers and nephews waited until after the game, when most of the crowd had left the stadium and—with no guards around—scattered Dad's ashes on home plate.

The morning after Kelsey arrived at our Seattle apartment for her grandfather's memorial service, she spent hours weeping. "Are you crying for Papa B?" I asked.

"Yes," she said, between sobs, "but also for our old house. I hate this apartment. The dark, fake-wood cabinets in the kitchen make it feel more like a motel than a home."

"Well, it's only for a year. And anyway, we have Marrowstone."

"But I haven't even *been to* the house on Marrowstone."

Kelsey cried when leaving the places and people she loved. When she flew from Seattle to New York City to start college, she wept throughout the entire five-plus-hour flight. A day or two later, she phoned me from New York. "Mom, you'll never guess where I am. Times Square! It is *so* amazing. I love this city so much. I can't believe I get to live here."

By the time Max turned up at our apartment after his overnight flight from Philadelphia, his short brown hair disheveled and his normally clear blue eyes red with fatigue, Kelsey was eager to go out with him for banh mi sandwiches in the International District. She mourned her losses, but her zest for living always prevailed over occasional bouts of melancholy.

The day before Dad's memorial service, my large extended family of Craig's and my children and my siblings, nieces, nephews, and cousins, accompanied us to Marrowstone so we could show them the house. We completed the three-hour trip—including a half-hour wait at the ferry terminal followed by a half-hour ferry ride—only to discover that our driveway was blocked by a fallen tree. Once the young adults had pushed the tree off the road, four cars filled with three generations of family members drove slowly up the long, curving driveway to our new home. After Craig unlocked the front door, Kelsey made straight for the kitchen with me close behind. "This looks like a country kitchen in France!" she exclaimed.

"That's exactly what your dad and I thought," I replied.

Craig and I had fallen in love with the house, in part, because the kitchen reminded us of France. When the kids were young, our family of five spent a few summers abroad, often cooking and eating in French country kitchens—red-tile floors, farmhouse sinks, and open cupboards—almost exactly like the kitchen in our Marrowstone house.

Our kids and their cousins tossed a Frisbee on East Beach and took photos of the Nordland General Store to send to their friends. "You're a country bumpkin now, Kelsey!" said her cousin Luke. She laughed. Despite my sadness over Dad's death, I was exultant that everyone, especially Kelsey, liked the house and the island. *This is only the beginning of many enjoyable times up here*, I thought.

The next day, back in Seattle, Kelsey and Luke gave the eulogy for Dad's service. His eyes on his daughter, Craig whispered to me, "I've never seen Kelsey looking so radiant."

"I know," I murmured. She was wearing a blue corduroy dress that set off her eyes, and she appeared stronger and more self-assured than she ever had. It was as though all the pieces of her had come to fit together perfectly.

Luke, who was, at the time, a member of the Coast Guard, wore his blond hair short in keeping with military regulations. His tucked-in shirt and pressed pants were a radical departure from the low-slung shorts and raggedy T-shirts he had favored as an adolescent. Because he was uncomfortable speaking in front of a group, he let Kelsey do most of the talking. They related experiences they'd shared with their grandpa over the years, especially during family reunions in Northern California and on more far-flung family trips to Chicago, the East Coast, and Europe. Kelsey concluded the eulogy by holding up a large box of donuts. "Papa B always thought that the best thing about donuts was being able to share them with others." Her smile was luminous.

Because Kelsey was catching a night flight back to Boston on the day after the service, she and I were able to go out for breakfast in Seattle. We shared an order of eggs and toast with the restaurant's legendary bacon jam and made plans to get together in Boston in a few weeks. "I've never been to Cape Cod, Mom. We can go there for a weekend after you meet my friends," Kelsey said finishing the last bite of her breakfast.

"I haven't been there either. It sounds perfect."

"And I want to spend more time at our home on Marrowstone," she announced.

My breath caught. My girl seemed to have made the transition from her childhood home to a place that promised to *become* home.

I often think of the last time I saw Kelsey, the last time I hugged her. I was sitting in a chair opposite the fireplace in our Seattle apartment. She walked toward me, her arms reaching out for an embrace, and smiled wistfully. "Goodbye, Mom. I love you. I'll call you tomorrow."

"I love you, too, sweetie," I replied. "I hate to see you go, but I'll talk to you tomorrow, and I'll see you again soon." I embraced her long enough to breathe in the spicy scent of her hair, the clean fragrance of her neck, the slight mustiness of her sweater.

chapter seven

My Mom

I wanted to inform my mom of Kelsey's death in person, not over the phone. So, after getting the news, Craig and I drove straight to her apartment in the retirement center. Mom opened the door wearing a stylish outfit, her white hair perfectly coiffed, her blue eyes filled with anguish. "I just heard that Kelsey was killed. Is that right? Can it be true?" Apparently, one of my cousins had already called her with the news.

I felt a burst of anger. "Oh, Mom, I wanted to tell you myself."

During the half-hour drive from her apartment to ours, she asked me again and again, "How did it happen?" Each time, I replied, "I don't know." As we neared our apartment building, she asked once more.

"I don't know, Mom. I don't know anything more than what I've already told you. Kelsey was killed in an accident involving a bus and a bike."

But Mom was asking about something other than the details of the accident. Her real question was: *How can this be happening to me* again? She'd just lost my dad, and years before that they'd both somehow endured the loss of my sister, Sally. As Mom sat, hunched and alone in the backseat of the car, I wished that my dad were there to support her through yet another crushing loss. Each of her questions made me feel like my skin was being torn from my body in strips. I wanted to scream, "Enough, Mom!" I wanted her to stop with the questions, but really, I wanted the universe to stop with inflicting pain.

Mom had suffered many bereavements, but perhaps the most life-changing of all was at age twelve when her mother died from a gunshot wound in an attempted robbery of their family grocery store in northern Illinois. Even though Mom had lived with her mother for twelve formative years, she had no memories of her. "None?" I asked in disbelief a few years after Kelsey died. "You can't remember her reading stories or singing songs to you? You can't remember her taking care of you when you were sick?" I couldn't fathom having no recollection of a mother's warmth and tender care.

But no, Mom couldn't remember anything. Mother-and-daughter relationships were especially charged for me. I couldn't bear the realization that Mom had no memories of her own mother—and I shuddered at the possibility of someday not being able to remember Kelsey.

I rummaged through boxes of family photographs, finding photos of the grandmother I never knew and hung them, framed, on the wall of Mom's apartment—one, a professional portrait from when my grandmother was about twenty; another, a photo of my grandparents in front of the rural Iowa church where they were married; and a third, a snapshot of my grandmother holding Mom when she was about one or so. I brought children's books and played songs from the 1920s when Mom was a child. "No," she responded when I asked whether the photos, books, or music had prompted a memory. "No, I don't remember anything, except maybe her saying a prayer with me before I went to bed."

"What was the prayer?" I asked, curious.

"The same one we taught you kids." I remembered that prayer. I'd said it every night as a child. But when I truly paid attention, the words startled me:

> *Now I lay me down to sleep.*
> *I pray the Lord my soul to keep.*
> *If I should die before I wake,*
> *I pray the Lord my soul to take.*

Had I paid attention to those alarming words when I said them each night of my childhood? Did I actually think I might die before the next morning? Maybe. Since Sally's death, my own death seemed a possibility, even if not imminent. The "Now I lay me down to sleep" prayer came from the eighteenth century, a time when children died much more frequently than now, the specter of death ever present. Even in the late nineteenth century when my grandparents were young, it wasn't uncommon for children to die: My grandmother lost three of her siblings in childhood; my grandfather lost two of his. Although I was grateful that the life-expectancy for my own children was so much longer, a thought crossed my mind: *I'd have felt less alone in my loss during my great grandparents' time.*

I remembered the nursery rhymes Mom taught me, the stories she read from the *Childcraft* book series, the lunches of tuna salad and peanut butter and jelly sandwiches she made for my picnics with the neighborhood kids. Because Mom was a nurse, our pediatrician instructed her to give me a penicillin shot in my butt whenever I had the croup—a remedy that was more embarrassing than painful. She always made up for it by buying me a book about Mrs. Piggle Wiggle book or the Bobbsey Twins in a series I adored. I gave the original *Mrs. Piggle-Wiggle* to Kelsey when she was about eight. "I loved this book," I told her. But she didn't like it.

"She isn't very nice, Mom."

"Who?"

"Mrs. Piggle-Wiggle."

"Why not? When I was a kid, I thought she was great."

"Well, she's not. She has terrible ideas about how to cure kids' problems. She told the parents of the little girl who didn't like to eat to cut her food into smaller and smaller pieces until they weren't giving her anything. The little girl could have starved!"

I reread the book and had to agree. Why had I so enjoyed it as a kid? I didn't even think about giving Kelsey one of the Bobbsey Twins books.

Even though Mom was at an impressionable age when she lost her mother—and even though she had suffered the illness and death of her own child—she somehow found her way to happiness. I wanted to know how she'd done it, but I was barely able to talk let alone pose the question.

chapter eight
Sacred Space

"The police say Kelsey may have been hit by more than one vehicle," announced our nephew Benj, stepping into our bedroom during that horrible afternoon after we'd learned of Kelsey's death. I looked up at him from my pillow, wondering briefly how he happened to be in touch with the Boston police, but I didn't have the energy to ask the question or even the desire to know the answer. His words seemed more part of an ongoing nightmare than reality. All day, I'd been trying to block images of Kelsey's lifeless body on a street in Boston. Even though the news added an element of horror, I didn't have the strength to protest. As much as I wanted to end the nightmare, it was far beyond my ability to do so.

I sat next to Craig on our midnight flight to Boston. Sam was seated across the aisle, kitty-corner from us. My brother-in-law had booked the flight and, either because of his careful seat selection or just plain luck, Craig and I had an empty seat in our row and Sam was alone in his. My friend Lise had packed my carry-on bag. "You'll probably need some dressy clothes to wear in Boston," she'd said as she searched for something suitable among the unpacked boxes in the bedroom closet. "I'm packing clothes for warm and cold weather. You never know what to expect on the East Coast in June." As far as I was concerned, the jeans and sweater I'd put on that morning, though it seemed like a lifetime ago, were all I'd need for the rest of my life.

The plane's interior lights dimmed during takeoff, and the thunder of its engines matched the tempest inside me. My world soon narrowed to our three seats—dark leather upholstery, the window shade drawn, and no one else visible in the almost completely dark plane. Craig and I unbuckled our seat belts to wrap our arms around each other. Like a bird trying to land in a gale, I couldn't settle. My head sometimes rested on Craig's lap, sometimes against his shoulder, and at one point I crouched on the floor in front of him, clutching his legs as he wrapped his arms around my shoulders. I asked him to repeat again and again the words he had spoken earlier in the day: "Nothing is ultimately lost but is gathered into God's infinite care and returned to us as possibility." His words saved me from tumbling into a free-fall. Although I sometimes looked over at Sam, I wasn't aware of anyone else on the plane.

When I'd discovered Sam was going to Boston with us, I was astounded. I hadn't expected it. I knew immediately after the call from the Boston Police that I needed to be in the city where Kelsey had taken her last breath—it was crucial for me as her mom—and I understood without asking that Craig would feel the same way. But I was too bound up in pain to grasp that it was important as well for both of her brothers.

Apparently, everyone except me realized there were also many practical reasons for traveling to Boston—to identify her body, make arrangements for cremation, pack up her room, and meet with her friends and teachers—but I wasn't thinking about any of that. Relief washed over me when I heard that Sam was accompanying us, but far more important than his practical support was his presence. I didn't know what it meant to be the mother of a child who had died—that was a tangle I couldn't even begin to loosen—but I was still Sam and Max's mom.

I think I asked Sam how he was doing—maybe in our apartment on Saturday night as we got ready to leave or in the waiting area before boarding the plane—but I'm not entirely sure. Although I worried that his caring for us might be a way to postpone his own anguish, I knew he needed to deal with difficult emotions in his own way.

When he was a baby, I spent hours trying to rock and sing him to sleep like I'd done with Kelsey when she was the same age. None of my comforting worked and, in fact, it made him fuss more. When I finally placed him in his crib and let him toss and turn on his own, he fell asleep within minutes, providing a valuable lesson that was reinforced throughout his growing-up years. As a preadolescent, he took his anger outside to shoot baskets, and as an older teenager, he withdrew to his room each time his football team lost—he was an offensive tackle and a defensive end on a team that lost a lot. When self-nurturing wasn't enough, he frequently asked Craig and me for help. Even though I was certain he could use our support now, Kelsey's death had sundered our usual ways of being with one another.

Craig helped Sam navigate the route to Boston College from the passenger seat of the car we'd rented at Logan Airport, while I leaned against the back window, staring at passing streets, aware that my daughter had been killed on one of them but not wanting to know the details. Just before we reached the college, Sam glanced at me in the rearview mirror and said, cautiously as if uncertain how I would respond, "I talked with Kelsey's friend Ada. She and Kelsey went to a reception at the art museum in the afternoon before the accident and then to dinner at a Mexican restaurant."

He checked to see if I was paying attention. I caught his eye and nodded, so he continued, "After dinner, Kelsey gave her jacket to Ada, since Ada wasn't dressed for the cold night. They said goodbye and headed off in different directions, but seconds later, something caused Ada to turn back." He took a deep breath before going on, "Ada saw Kelsey lying on the ground and immediately knew she was dead. But—and this is what comforts me—she said that Kelsey looked peaceful."

I was grateful Sam had been consoled by Ada's words, but I tried to push them away. The image of Kelsey lying motionless on a street was harrowing. Instead, I reflected on a moment soon after her birth. A nurse had bathed her, coaxed her abundant hair into a sweet curl on top of her head, and positioned her in my arms. As I clasped my new baby close to my heart, she looked up at me, her eyes filled with wonder, and my heart burst with a love stronger than anything I'd ever experienced. I tried to give her the best of me. She was, to quote the British poet W.H. Auden, "my north, my south, my east and west." *Was that for nothing? Where did all that love go?* I wondered.

When we reached Boston College, a Jesuit university in Chestnut Hill outside of Boston, Sam phoned the campus minister, and a few minutes later Father MacMillan, gray haired and slightly stooped, met us in front of the dormitory where the college had offered us rooms. The three of them, Father MacMillan, Sam, and Craig, chatted for a while, but even though I was standing right next to them, I couldn't comprehend their conversation which seemed mostly pleasantries that made no sense. I ached for the priest to take us to a chapel—*maybe I can find Kelsey there*—but I couldn't even speak.

It was just after dawn on a Sunday morning, and the dormitory was silent. There were no sounds from the rooms, no trucks rumbling by outside, no students on the pathways leading from the dorm to classrooms. The emptiness seemed fitting; the rest of the world no longer existed for me. In the lobby, a cascade of empty beer cans flowed from a garbage can to the floor. In the elevator, packets of unused condoms lay next to soggy notebook paper and even more beer cans. "Saturday night at the end of the school year is a pretty rowdy time," Father MacMillan said apologetically. I looked around at the detritus of a raucous night on campus and suddenly saw the space around me in an extraordinary way, more like the chapel I had yearned to visit than a muddy, garbage-strewn elevator. A voice that was both in my head and seemingly from outside of me, proclaimed, *Life continues!* While I didn't know if *my* life could continue, I found strength in the unflagging continuation of the life force—that which drives salmon to spawn in their natal streams, compels seven or eight generations of monarch butterflies to complete a single circuit of migration, and causes young adults to carouse on a Saturday night. When the elevator door opened, I walked toward our dormitory suite with a heavy heart but a tad lighter step.

Two sets of bunk beds and four dressers filled the suite's bedroom. A miniscule kitchen with a table, refrigerator, and two-burner stove was adjacent to the living room. A bank of leaded glass windows in the living room faced what, through the mist, resembled a medieval castle but was just another Boston College dorm. A long brown couch was pushed against a wall, with a vase of fresh daisies on the shelf across from it. I put the small photograph that I always carried in my wallet—our three kids on a hillside bench overlooking Lake Union with the Seattle skyline in the background—next to the flowers.

Max and his cousin Luke, haggard from the melancholy drive from New York, arrived midmorning. Max had left Swarthmore on Saturday afternoon, after learning of Kelsey's death, and taken a train to New York City, where Luke lived. I hugged them but could say little beyond, "I love you." Love was the only thing that still made sense. I went into the bedroom and climbed on a top bunk, reasoning that the higher I was, the more likely I'd somehow *find* my daughter. Although exhausted, I was afraid to fall asleep, fearful that sleep might bring temporary amnesia. I was terrified of having to learn—all over again—that Kelsey was dead.

Max and Sam went to identify Kelsey's body at the police morgue. In the weeks that followed, I asked myself why I didn't go instead of them. I'd seriously considered doing so, but Craig and our friends warned me: "If you go, you'll have the image of her lifeless body in your head forever." While I didn't know where Kelsey was, I knew she wasn't in the morgue. A couple of days later, I asked Max what Kelsey's body had looked like. He pointed to the battered ring she'd worn at the time of the accident, which we retrieved at the time of the accident. "Kind of like that ring." I was glad I hadn't gone but immensely sorry Sam and Max had to see her lifeless body.

Late that afternoon, the sun obscured by heavy clouds, Craig accompanied Sam and Max to the funeral home to arrange for cremation. I was alone in the suite, looking out the windows from the living room couch, when my when my phone pinged. It was a text from Pam, a close friend and former neighbor whose three kids were almost the same ages as ours. The text contained a link to two songs by Debbie Friedman. Both songs, first sung in Hebrew and then in English, were renditions of traditional Jewish prayers. "Elohai N'Shamah" is translated as "My God, the soul that you have given me is pure." The translation for "Mi Shebeirach," a prayer for the sick and grieving, is "May the source of strength who blessed the ones before us, help us find the courage to make our lives a blessing."

I switched on a lamp next to the couch so that I could see the photograph of the kids and listened to the songs over and over again. The sung prayers seemed to be telling me that Kelsey still existed— and that there was a "source of strength" that would help me through this unbearable loss. Gradually, the muted voice in my head that had been repeating *Kelsey is dead* for the past twenty-four hours subsided, and for a few precious moments, I no longer wondered, *Where is she?* She was with me. I couldn't touch the softness of her skin or see the light in her eyes, but there was a fullness in my chest, a sensation of being ever so lightly caressed. And words came into my head: *Mom, I am so, so sorry. I know how hard this is for you, but you'll find your way through the pain.* I believed the words to be the invention of my grief-crazed imagination—but, even so, they were consoling. Before he left that evening to return to New York, our nephew Luke glanced around the dorm room and murmured, "This feels like sacred space." It felt that way to me, too.

chapter nine

Boston

"I want you to know that Kelsey's last weekend was very special," said Ginny, standing by the arched doorway that separated the living room from the rest of the apartment. She smiled, her eyes glistening with tears, and brushed back her shoulder-length blonde hair. Kelsey and Ginny had met in Boston through a mutual friend the autumn before. Both of them were fascinated by psychology, loved to travel, and devoted an inordinate amount of time exploring their feelings. They spent many weekends together, keeping a few clothes in each other's apartment. I could barely wrap my mind around the finality of "last weekend," but I did want to hear about it.

Kelsey had talked about her Boston friends during phone calls and visits home. "You know how I didn't think I had much in common with the other students in my program?" she said a few months before her death. "They seemed so young, and I missed my friends from New York, but something happened second semester. Somehow, I opened up to them and saw how smart and funny they really are."

Her Boston friends had reached out to Sam to extend an invitation to their gathering. "I think it'll be helpful for us—and for them—if we're there," Sam declared. So, that night, after Luke left to return to New York, Sam drove Craig, Max, and me to the apartment of one of Kelsey's graduate school friends, a young man who greeted us at the door with such a fearful look on his face, I thought he must be terrified of both our despair and *his own*. He led us into the living room. Several people who'd been sitting on armchairs or sprawling on the rug stood up to greet us. "We're so glad you came tonight," said a small, dark-haired girl with a warm smile. The others nodded. I sat down on an empty couch and looked at the sad but

them with her friends but wanted my input as well. I don't remember having strong feelings one way or another, but I do remember that listening to her debate options made me feel like I was in the middle of a sunny meadow rather than parked on a rainy Seattle street. A week later, she accepted a position in another college's counseling center, because she liked the staff and was excited about working with college students. As her graduate-school friends spoke about how Kelsey had helped them, I knew she'd made the right choice—but I also felt the sadness of what would never be.

The next morning, we drove to Kelsey's neighborhood in an old suburb of Boston near Boston College that teemed with bookstores, cafés, and students. Young people were everywhere: waiting at street corners for the light to change, chatting as they walked along the streets, and standing in line at coffee shops. Kelsey had told me about the area during a phone call the summer before.

"Hi, Mom. Where are you?"

"In Chicago with your dad. He's at a meeting, and I'm at the Art Institute, sitting next to a gorgeous fountain in the courtyard café and drinking coffee."

"Oh, I can picture that. I'm in Boston, looking for an apartment. There are so many more possibilities here than in New York."

"Have you found one you like?"

"I think so. It's in a neighborhood with lots of students and coffee shops, and I would have only one roommate—a woman from Australia who's getting her PhD in biology. I really like her."

"Are you going to take it?"

"I have to think about it for a while, but I'm pretty sure I will."

"You certainly don't want to rush into a decision!"

She laughed. "No danger of that."

Friends from Seattle who were in Boston for a college reunion offered to drive us to Kelsey's apartment. We'd planned to stop for breakfast along the way and chose a café with big windows and a long counter chock-full of pastries. "I bet Kelsey came here," I said to our friends the moment we walked inside. It was exactly the kind of place she liked: tables wide enough for her to spread out her books and computer, a steady supply of coffee, and windows that let in the sunlight. I imagined her finding a cozy spot and surrounded by her textbooks and the *New York Times,* staying there for hours. The next day, as Ginny and I passed by the café on our way to mail the boxes of Kelsey's belongings to Seattle, I asked her about it. "Yep," she replied, "she came here all the time—it was her favorite place to read and write!" She pointed to the table where Kelsey liked to sit, which was right next to the window, just as I had imagined.

After breakfast, we drove to Kelsey's apartment building—a red-brick structure surrounding a leafy courtyard. I'd never visited her there, although earlier in the year, I'd suggested flying to Boston to help celebrate her Saint Patrick's Day birthday. She looked at me, her eyes widening. "Thanks, Mom, but I've already made plans with my friends." Apparently sensing my disappointment, she quickly added, "But come this summer after I finish school."

Kelsey's roommate, Shelley, opened the door to the apartment. "I'm sorry," she said, tucking a strand of light brown hair behind her ear and dabbing her eyes with a tissue. "I just learned about Kelsey. I was gone all weekend, and now I can't stop crying."

"Me either." I said, gently reaching out to touch her arm. "We wanted to meet you before the others get here." Sam, Max, Ginny, and several of Kelsey's friends had volunteered to pack up Kelsey's possessions.

"Maybe you'd like some time by yourselves in her room?" Shelley suggested to Craig and me. In Kelsey's bedroom, almost everything—the green-and-ivory embroidered pillow from a trip she and her cousin Melissa had taken to India, a large poster of the Brooklyn Bridge, a photo of Sam and Max from a family trip—was familiar. As Craig looked around the room, the color drained from his face. "I can't stay here," he said and bolted for the door. I stretched out on her bed and buried my face in her pillow. I could catch traces of her scent, which intensified my yearning. *Oh, Kelsey, why can't you just walk in and sit down next to me?* The room was tidy: no clothes strewn on the chair, no books on the floor, no papers covering her desk—so unlike the childhood bedroom she reclaimed whenever she came home for a visit. *Did some part of you know we would be here?* I shivered. Anything seemed possible. The room was filled with objects Kelsey loved—but *she* wasn't there. I pushed myself off her bed and walked over to her dresser, my eyes drawn to a folded paisley scarf I'd seen her wear on so many occasions. I wrapped it around my shoulders and left the room.

Sam and Max, along with Kelsey's friends, were standing near the door to her bedroom, waiting to begin the packing. "Is it okay if we start?" Sam asked.

My heart filled with sorrow—I hated that he and Max had to pack up Kelsey's belongings. I nodded. "Your dad and I don't need any more time in the bedroom." Even though I wished they didn't have to go through this painful task, I knew that I couldn't bear to do the sorting and boxing.

Back in the living room, I took a seat on the empty sofa. Muted sunlight filtered through the windows and onto the carpet. "Is there anything of Kelsey's that you'd like?" I asked, turning to Shelley.

She thought for a moment. "I'd like her teapot unless you want it." She walked to the kitchen counter and held up the pot. "It'll remind me of the many times we had tea together."

I'd spotted the ceramic teapot, glazed in a forest green hue and with three, large pink roses entwined around the handle, in a trendy Seattle store while Christmas shopping a few years earlier and had immediately known Kelsey would love it.

"Please keep it, Shelley," I replied. "It'll do my heart good to think of you using it."

I made room on the sofa for Ada, who had chosen to stay in the living room instead of helping pack up Kelsey's belongings. I said, quietly, "You and I are like bookends." She nodded. I wasn't sure she knew what I meant, so I added, "I was with Kelsey when she was born, and you were with her when she died."

I knew Ada wasn't physically with Kelsey when she died—no one was. Despite trying to block images of her death, I couldn't help reflecting on that moment. I wondered whether Kelsey had seen the bus coming. I wondered whether she'd been scared. I considered asking Ada, *What made you turn around after you left Kelsey?* But the question was too fraught for both of us. About a year later, I asked Ginny, "Why do you think Ada turned to look for Kelsey after the accident? What made her do it?"

Ginny thought for a moment and then replied, "She had a strong feeling." *What <u>was</u> that feeling?* I wondered. (I've continued to wonder about it, but even if I were to ask Ada now, the passage of time— and the impact of trauma—might well have obscured her memories. And what would be the point of reigniting a thunderbolt of pain?)

After leaving the apartment, Craig, Sam, Max, and I drove downtown to meet with an attorney who was helping us sort through the intricacies of the police investigation. We sat around a large table, rain pounding against the lone window, the sky a blanket of gray. My disposition matched the wretched weather as I tried to absorb what the attorney was telling us. It was difficult to concentrate. He told us—I had to check with Craig, Sam, and Max later for the details I'd missed—that several people saw Kelsey lying on the ground after the bus passed, one of them a nurse who rushed to perform CPR, but no one knew what actually happened. And then the attorney said, "The bus driver didn't stop."

My fogginess abruptly cleared, and my face felt hot. I spit out the words, *"Didn't stop?"*

He nodded. "The police had to track down the bus to question the driver."

I had imagined forgiving the driver—that the bus hadn't even stopped seemed outrageous—but then my shoulders slumped in resignation. I didn't have the strength for anger, and anyway, it would do nothing in the face of my daughter's death. It certainly wouldn't bring her back. An image flashed in my mind: five-year-old Kelsey, learning to ride her bike in front of our house, her hands gripping the handlebars, her face shining with excitement. The attorney interrupted my thoughts. "The police can't tell you anything about the accident during the investigation, and they probably won't have a report until the end of the summer."

I traced the grain of the tabletop with one finger and took a deep breath. What did it ultimately matter how the accident happened? The details would allow me to paint a mental picture of Kelsey's death, but that wasn't what was most important. I could let go of her physical presence—what choice did I have? But never in a million years could I let go of what tied us together or accept that my beautiful, vibrant Kelsey was lost to me forever.

After leaving the attorney's office, Craig and I went to a reception hosted by the Boston College Mental Health Counseling program. Students and faculty members were staggering in, having just finished a windy, rainy walk to honor Kelsey, leaving their umbrellas on the floor and draping their soggy coats over chairs. I walked over to the buffet of hot and cold hors d'oeuvres and waited my turn in line. I wasn't hungry, but standing in line gave me something to do. A middle-aged woman next to me introduced herself. "I adored Kelsey," she said. "She was one of my favorite students. But I must tell you, I'm a mother, and I'm surprised you are even able to stand."

That I could remain upright astonished me, too, but being around people who had known and loved Kelsey—seeing her through their eyes—made me feel closer to her. Each word of remembrance softened my heartache and made it slightly more bearable. I thanked the woman and stepped away from the buffet line. Sam was chatting with Kelsey's advisor—Kelsey had planned to accompany her to Guatemala the next month to interview Indigenous women—and Max was engaged in a conversation with a group of students who wanted our family's permission to erect a "ghost bike," a bicycle painted all-white to commemorate the death of a cyclist. (We granted permission, and the ghost bike remained at the site of Kelsey's accident for over a year.)

A Black woman who appeared to be in her late thirties approached me. Her somber face and penetrating eyes resembled those of a figure in an El Greco painting. "I was on vacation," she said, "but I hurried back to Boston when I got the news. I needed to be here." I nodded, and she continued, "Kelsey was in my class first semester. I was new to the college, not very confident, and your daughter helped me more than I can say. I'm so sorry for your loss."

Kelsey had told me about this professor who knew a lot about her subject but had difficulty connecting with her students. Most of the students had given up on her, but not Kelsey, who scheduled an appointment during the professor's office hours. One conversation led to another, and their meetings continued into the next semester, even though Kelsey was no longer one of her students. The professor didn't realize how transformative these discussions were for Kelsey. She told me during a visit home, "I was nervous around my high school teachers, and I hadn't been able to talk to my college professors when I disagreed with them. But I told this professor exactly what I thought was wrong with her teaching."

"Really, Kelsey? That was gutsy," I responded.

"She knew a lot of important stuff we needed to learn," Kelsey added, "but she didn't know how to teach it. When she got to know us, as real people and not just names on a list, her teaching was so much better."

A young Turkish woman wearing a hijab told me, "Kelsey and I worked together on the college's refugee project. We spent a lot of time talking about our classes, our families, all kinds of things. I can't tell you how much I'm going to miss her."

A robust Black man with what seemed to be an African accent and wearing a clerical collar—closer to my age than to Kelsey's—told me, "Kelsey and I often talked about religion. She was a very spiritual woman." His words shocked me. I'd never thought of Kelsey as "spiritual"—she had absolutely no interest in attending a church of any kind except for joining the family for Christmas Eve services. When I told Sam that I'd been taken aback by the priest's comment, he stared at me in amazement. "Mom! How can you be surprised? She didn't go to church, but she was *very* spiritual."

Sam's comment startled me. Why hadn't I thought of Kelsey as "spiritual"? All at once, an image came to mind of the day when Craig, Max, and I visited her workplace in the South Bronx. Youth Ministries for Peace and Justice, a nonprofit agency in the South Bronx, is dedicated to rebuilding surrounding neighborhoods by coaching community members to become "prophetic voices for peace and justice." As the agency's youth advocate, Kelsey had a multifaceted job: tutoring high school students; meeting with their teachers and school administrators; advocating, along with her students, for restorative justice in their high school; and implementing a high school degree program for her students' parents. Every Friday afternoon, the agency staff held a discussion on the Gospel's message of liberation. Craig, Max, and I were there for one of those discussions. After it concluded, Kelsey led us to the fellowship hall of the Catholic church next door and, with evident pride, drew our attention to a mural that covered an entire wall. "Do you know what this is about?" she asked.

"Well, I'm pretty sure that's Jesus," Craig said, pointing to long-haired man in a white robe, one arm upraised in a blessing.

"Yeah, you can't mistake him for just a random passerby," Kelsey said, smiling. "But do you know where he is?"

"In a river with a city burning all around it. Is it the South Bronx?"

"Yep. It's the Bronx River. The mural was painted in the 1970s when one building after another was burning in the South Bronx.

That's when the founder created this agency. The kids helped paint the mural and included themselves in it—some of them wading in the river, not far from Jesus, and others onshore."

"It's wonderful, Kelsey," said Craig. "I'm so glad you brought us to see it. It seemed to me that this afternoon's discussion was rooted in liberation theology." When Craig was a seminary student in Chicago, living with a Black street gang, he'd been inspired by the writings of North American liberation theologists, such as Dr. Martin Luther King, Jr., and by the work of Central American liberation theologists, primarily Jesuit priests, who proclaimed that Jesus's message of "good news to the poor" was crucial in the struggle against racism, tyranny, and domination.

"We talk about liberation theology every week," Kelsey responded. "It goes hand in hand with the writings of Paulo Freire, the Brazilian educator whose books I read in college. Our Friday afternoon discussions make me feel better about Christianity, at least the way it's practiced by liberation theologists."

Throughout our days in Boston, I'd been receiving texts from relatives and friends who were accompanying me in my sorrow. *Where are you, now?* texted my friend, Pam.

Holding Kelsey's ashes, and waiting for the train to New York, I texted back.

Pam sent me a poem by Emily Dickinson, the last stanza of which was riveting:

This is the Hour of Lead –
Remembered, if outlived,
As Freezing persons, recollect the Snow –
First - Chill – then Stupor – then the letting go –

"Hour of Lead" accurately expressed how I was feeling as I held the bag containing Kelsey's ashes in my arms and looked out the train window at the gray skies and cold drizzle of Boston. The words, "chill" and "stupor," were also right on target—but "letting go"? No. I was well aware of how much I'd been forced to let go of, but I resisted the active process of *letting go.* In fact, I was running in the opposite direction, determined to *not* let go of my relationship with Kelsey.

As the train left Boston on the way to New York City, I placed the bag with Kelsey's ashes on the floor in front of me and picked up a book I'd purchased at the station: *New and Selected Poems* by Mary Oliver. I was hopeful Mary Oliver's poetry would help me find my way to Kelsey, but I hit a roadblock in her beautiful, but to me troubling poem, "In Blackwater Woods." Oliver writes about what it means to be mortal: we love deeply what is mortal and then, when the time comes, we let it go. Her words left me feeling alone and confused. *What does Mary Oliver really know about the pain of losing a child*, I wondered. But I read the disquieting lines over and over until finally I realized that while Oliver is writing about the most fundamental of all human dilemmas, she isn't saying we have to let go of love, rather the mortal nature of that which we love. The loss of Kelsey's physical being was excruciating, heartrending, and awful—but I had resigned myself to it, or at least I was on my way to doing so. What I could never, ever let go of was our connectedness.

chapter ten
Priest Lake and Memories

I found myself remembering *bat time*, the moment right before dark when tiny bats suddenly appeared above us on the deck of Craig's parents' Priest Lake cabin in northern Idaho, their fleeting forms illuminated by the lights of the cabin. *Why am I remembering bat time now?* I wondered as the train headed for New York, but later I understood: Memories can be metaphors, much like those in a dream. In the early days of grief, memories of Kelsey and moments of feeling connected to her were ephemeral, brief, and transitory— like bat time at Priest Lake.

Each summer while our kids were growing up, we drove seven hours from Seattle to join Craig's parents, his three siblings, and their children on Priest Lake. With its high rafters, an enormous stone fireplace, and an assortment of beds, the cabin was large enough to accommodate all of us. We often joined Craig's mom on the wrap-around deck that overlooked the lake to watch the sun set and wait for bats.

The deep blue lake, fed by streams from the Selkirk Mountains and surrounded by forests of pine, spruce, and hemlock, stretched for miles through the northernmost portion of Idaho. Frigid in early June, the water wasn't swimmable until midsummer. Some of the kids got up soon after dawn and raced down the dock, whooping as they flung themselves into the icy water. In the early afternoons, I usually took a novel to the end of the dock, occasionally lifting my head above its pages to watch as our kids and their cousins cavorted in the water and messed about with canoes. When I was too hot and sweaty to continue reading, I jumped into the chilly water, swam a few laps between our dock and the neighbor's, and then joined the kids in the fun of rolling the canoes.

Most summers, we took one or two canoe trips, once to Upper Priest in Canada, but we usually opted instead for short outings in Idaho. On one overnight trip, when nine of us—seven kids and two adults—were camping on a small island in the lake, an unexpected thunderstorm abruptly ended our adventure. Thunderstorms on Priest Lake were awe-inspiring: sudden torrential rain, deafening thunder, and lightning bolts that sometimes struck the tall pines surrounding the cabin. Craig's sister hammered the power boat across cresting waves to rescue us, and we clambered aboard, crowding into the stern and leaving behind our soggy tents and canoes.

We often drove into the mountains northeast of the cabin to search for huckleberries, picking them until we had enough for a pie and for pancakes the next morning too. As I thought about huckleberry picking, an image came into my head of Kelsey, about ten at the time, wearing a purple baseball cap atop her sun-bleached hair, her too-large Priest Lake T-shirt covering her knees as she bends to pick the tiny berries and plop them into a container.

At least once a summer, we ventured farther up mountain to cascading pools fed by an icy stream, jumped into the lowest pool, staying submerged until our bodies tingled, then scrambled out to warm ourselves on the sunny rocks. Often, we returned to the grassy knolls where wild huckleberries grew in abundance and resumed picking until the afternoon sun forced us to stop. It felt delicious to return to the cabin—dusty, hot, and sticky with huckleberry juice— and then race into the water of the cold, clear lake.

Each year, upon returning to Seattle after weeks spent at Priest Lake, Kelsey lay on her bed, wearing her favorite Priest Lake sweatshirt and quietly weeping. One year, having listened to her gentle sobs for longer that I could stand, I taped a stanza of "The Lake Isle of Innisfree" by the nineteenth-century, Irish poet William Butler Yeats, over her bed:

I will arise and go now, for always night and day
I hear lake water lapping with low sounds by the
shore;
While I stand on the roadway, or on the pavements
grey,
I hear it in the deep heart's core.

Before Kelsey's death, whenever I remembered our nights and days on Priest Lake, I could almost hear "lake water lapping with low sounds by the shore," almost put myself back into the moment of returning from the mountains and jumping into the lake. But on the train ride between Boston and New York—knowing that Kelsey would never again swim in a mountain-fed lake, gather huckleberries, or watch for bat time—the memories made me feel as bleak as a fire ravaged forest.

I couldn't stand the thought that memories were all I had left of Kelsey. After she died, many well-wishers said to me, "May her memory be a blessing." Although I knew the words were said to provide comfort, whenever I heard them I inwardly screamed, *I want so much more than memories!*

In her book, *The Path of Blessing: Experiencing the Energy and the Abundance of the Divine,* Rabbi Marcia Prager defines *blessing* this way: "to move something of myself toward you." Eventually, I came up with a paraphrase that retained the beauty and kindness of the original phrase, while also expressing my longing for a beyond-the-grave relationship with Kelsey. Whenever someone said to me, "May her memory be a blessing," I translated it in my head as: *May your memory of Kelsey move that which is deepest in her toward you and that which is deepest in you toward her.* I welcomed *that* blessing.

chapter eleven
New York

"Isn't it beautiful, Mom," Kelsey exclaimed, looking across the Columbia campus—Barnard is a women's college within Columbia University—toward the city beyond. She hadn't lived in New York for long, only a few months, and I was visiting her for the first time since Craig and I had helped her move into her freshman dorm. As we sat together on the library steps, I scanned the Manhattan skyline, perceiving mostly steel, concrete, and rooftop water tanks, but Kelsey saw something that made her heart soar.

"It's impressive," I responded, "but I don't think New York is 'beautiful.' For me that word is reserved for nature—trees, mountains, oceans, sky—and maybe for Paris."

"Oh no, I don't agree with you. I think this city is gorgeous. I love the lines, the lights, the energy. I love knowing that in all these buildings, there are people trying to figure out how to live their lives."

The first time I visited Kelsey in Brooklyn, several years after her graduation from college, we met in Midtown Manhattan and traveled together to her apartment. Following a thirty-minute ride on a crowded subway and a subsequent walk on streets that grew increasingly more dystopian—austere buildings, fewer and fewer trees, more and more liquor stores—we arrived at her apartment house. "This is it, Mom," she announced. Covered with asphalt shingles and bare of vegetation, the building seemed straight out of the Great Depression. But when I glanced at Kelsey, anticipation dancing in her eyes, I could see that she wasn't the least bit apologetic. I was amazed, not so much by the dreariness of the building—I'd lived in similar ones—but by Kelsey. She really did have an aesthetic informed by the inner life: not only of human beings but also of cities and structures. Rather than drab siding and barren landscape, she saw energy, light, and love.

When the train from Boston entered Penn Station—during that hellish week after Kelsey had died—my stomach churned. *Can I bear the memories this city holds?* I wondered. But then, we stepped out of the station and into sunshine following days of rain, and I felt like Persephone emerging from the netherworld. As our taxi wound through the crowded streets on the way to our nephew Luke's apartment in Brooklyn, I even smiled. This rich and vibrant place had been Kelsey's home for four years of college and five subsequent years of working in the city. Her love for New York seemed to radiate from every building, traffic light, and passerby.

Katie, who was Kelsey's closest friend and her roommate for many of the years my daughter had lived in New York, texted me: *I want to see you, and I want to be part of your family always.*

You will be, I texted back. *And someday I'll dance at your wedding.* I couldn't dance at my own daughter's wedding—that realization had come like a kick in the gut repeatedly over the past days—but I could dance at Katie's.

The two young women had met in the spring of 2002, when they were in New York to attend Barnard's weekend for accepted students to get to know the campus. Kelsey hadn't been particularly interested in applying to the college. That Barnard was a women-only school didn't appeal to her, nor could she imagine living in such a large and frenetic city. She'd submitted the application fueled by her dad's enthusiasm for the school and then erased it from her mind. When people asked her about the schools she'd applied to, she usually forgot to mention Barnard. Her acceptance letter came with an invitation for the April 2002 weekend event. "That's great, Kelsey," I said when she showed it to me.

"Yeah. I'm shocked. I wasn't expecting this at all," she replied.

"Are you interested in Barnard?"

She shook her head. "I don't think so, but I haven't thought about it. I've been focused on my other applications."

"So, what about visiting it again?" I prodded. "It would be fabulous to spend a week with you in New York. It'll be spring break for both of us." My job didn't bring in big bucks, but one of the perks was having the same vacation dates as our kids.

Kelsey's eyes shone. She was always eager to travel. "That sounds like fun, but I don't want you, Dad, or anyone else to think I'm committing to Barnard because I am *not*."

During our entire week in New York, the sky was as blue and clear as the water of Priest Lake. It was the middle of April, and as we walked through Central Park we could see tender green leaves on the trees, pink and purple flowers poking up through the ground, and every few yards, a cluster of bright yellow daffodils growing from bulbs planted the previous fall after the terrorist attack of September 11. The limestone facade of the Metropolitan Museum of Art gleamed in the sunlight, but we spent an entire afternoon inside, delving into the Impressionist and Egyptian collections. The next day, we walked to the chateau-like New York Public Library at Forty-Second Street and Fifth Avenue and sat on a nearby park bench eating hot dogs slathered with sauerkraut and onions. Small ripples of pleasure ran down my spine. I was in New York City, eating hot dogs in the sunshine with my girl.

Brooklyn was also on our itinerary. During the early seventies when I was a student at New York University in Greenwich Village, not far from Brooklyn, the borough had seemed so remote and uninteresting that I never, not even once, ventured there. In the city once again, this time with my eighteen-year-old daughter, I suggested that we visit Brooklyn. Both of us were interested in the Hasidic communities that had taken root in the Borough Park neighborhood, so we decided to take the subway there. Secularism was a threat to Hasidism even before the Second World War, but subsequent to the Holocaust, the surviving Hasidim were determined to live at a remove from the rest of the world so as to preserve their religious life. Few places were as indicative of this as Borough Park. Although we couldn't go to a Hasidic shul—synagogue and school—and we had no way of being invited into a private home where much of Hasidic life took place, we did attempt to get a sense of community by listening and observing in the streets, stores, and restaurants. We were fascinated by the people we encountered: wig-wearing women pushing baby carriages and trailed by numerous children in matching clothes, men with side curls beneath flat Hasidic hats who assiduously avoided eye contact with us, and clusters of animated teen-agers in school uniforms. While eating kosher pizza, we overheard a group of high school girls discussing what they wanted to do after graduation. As far as we could discern, their choices were limited to marriage or a year of working before marriage.

Kelsey was interested in the broad concept of *community*. She'd written articles for her high school newspaper about various ethnic communities in Seattle and eventually made studying cities and communities her major focus at Barnard. When I visited her during her sophomore year, she asked, "Mom, do you want to go with me to the headquarters of the Jehovah's Witnesses in Brooklyn? The young members who assist in the publication of their magazine *Watchtower* live as well as work there, and I want to interview a few of the women."

"Sure, I'd love to go with you," I replied.

The elevated train swayed on the bridge between Manhattan and Brooklyn, as Kelsey and I clung tightly to a metal pole. Outside the window, a tall building with WATCHTOWER in large red-neon letters loomed into view. "That's where we're going," Kelsey said.

"Hmm. Do you think the women will tell you what they really think about their community?"

"I don't know. Maybe not. But I hope I can get a feel for the place. I have so many questions written down and even more in my head."

The racially diverse women Kelsey interviewed were proud of their work on the Bible-based magazine. Kelsey spoke at length with a young Black woman and then asked if there were children in the Watchtower community. "No," the woman answered, a glimmer of sadness in her eyes. "I'm married, and when my husband and I have children, we'll have to leave." Her response saddened Kelsey as well.

By the time Kelsey graduated from college, she had conversed with people in various community organizations throughout the city and completed internships in a few of them. "I'm not sure what I'll do next," she informed me as her graduation drew close, "but I want to be part of a group of people trying to make a difference."

Toward the end of that week in New York during Kelsey's senior year of high school, we purchased a cheap sleeping bag at Morris

Brothers on Broadway and walked the few blocks to Barnard. Kelsey met up with the other students, and I joined a question-and-answer session for parents, sitting down next to a woman from Long Island. Since this was only six months after the September 11 attacks, she asked if I was brave enough to send my daughter to school in New York City. "Aren't you afraid of another terrorist attack?" I shook my head. I was certain my daughter was *not* going to attend school in New York, confident that she had no intention of becoming a Barnard student.

Kelsey and I had planned to meet well before the official end of the event, figuring that would be more than enough time. At the agreed-upon hour, I walked through the wrought iron gate to the foyer of the red-brick administrative building. The instant I saw my daughter's glowing face, I perceived a shift in the energy field surrounding her. "Hi, Mom!" she called, bounding down the stairs to greet me. "I want to stay. I'm really having a good time." My heart contracted with the sudden consciousness that Kelsey was no longer a child but instead a young woman ready to make her way in the world—and from the look on her face, I suspected that would include Barnard. I crossed the street and sat on the steps of Low Library to phone Craig. "I'm not surprised," he said after I'd shared my premonition that Kelsey would choose Barnard.

"Why is that?" I asked. "I'm shocked."

"I always thought she'd like Barnard once she spent a little more time there. Can you imagine what an education she'll get just from living in the city?"

"I thought she'd be intimidated by New York. She was when we visited last year." I recalled the dialogue we'd had in a coffee shop on the Upper West Side at the end of her junior year of high school. "I like New York," she'd said, "but it scares me to think of actually going to school here."

Craig continued our conversation. "Haven't you done your best this week to show her how much fun New York can be?"

Both Katie and Kelsey decided to attend Barnard, but even though they'd shared a dinner during that weekend event, they saw little of each other during their first semester. They did, however, spend a Saturday at the beginning of second semester walking around various New York neighborhoods. They enjoyed that day so much that they devoted almost every subsequent Saturday or Sunday to scoping out the lesser-known corners of the city. They lived together their sophomore and senior years and shared an apartment in Brooklyn after graduation.

Kelsey had planned to help celebrate Katie's twenty-eighth birthday in New York—but of course, she never made it. Katie's dad, Peter, flew to New York from Chicago to join in the celebration—but instead, he spent the weekend helping Katie cope with her best friend's death. Soon after we arrived at Luke's Brooklyn apartment, Katie and Peter joined us. As they walked in the door, Peter asked if we wanted to hear a few "Katie and Kelsey stories." "I hope so," he said, "because they're really funny."

"Okay," I responded, a bit confused. I'd expected tears, not Katie telling us funny stories. But in spite of that, the stories made me laugh. Katie talked about how, a few days after graduation, she and Kelsey had trekked from the top of Manhattan to the bottom, passing through many of the neighborhoods they'd explored over the previous four years. Sunburned and with blisters on their feet, but enormously pleased with themselves, they hobbled back to their college-owned apartment and spent the rest of the night reminiscing.

Right before Katie left, I drew her aside and handed her Kelsey's favorite turquoise-and-silver ring. "It's perfect," she said, slightly above a whisper, grasping the ring tightly. "Even though I often thought of leaving New York, I want you to know that I'd never change the nine years I spent here with Kelsey for anything."

At about three in the morning, I awoke with a start and surveyed the darkened room. Craig was next to me in the bed, the top of his head just visible above the down comforter. I could distinguish Luke's bike hanging on the opposite wall and below it, the small Eddie Bauer backpack containing Kelsey's ashes. I grimaced, recognizing the inadvertent but ironic collocation of bicycle and ashes, but mostly I felt hollow. At that moment, a breeze redolent of seaweed drifted into the room and tickled my neck. *Where is it coming from?* I wondered. The only possibility seemed to be the window that doubled as a headboard for the bed. I passed my finger along the bottom of the window frame until I located the latch. It was firmly locked, and no air was trickling through. *Maybe it's Kelsey,* I thought. There was a gentleness about it that was reminiscent of her.

Then I recalled Katie's words from the evening before: "I wouldn't change the nine years I spent here with Kelsey for anything." I was struck by a moment of clarity: The stories Katie shared with us had been like drinking from a deep well, bringing Kelsey to life and making us laugh. Over the years they'd spent together in New York, the two young women explored not only the city but also their emotions, dreams, and aspirations—and they always found reasons to laugh. I felt a surge of gratitude for their extraordinary friendship and for their laughter, unconquerable even by death. With the breeze still caressing my neck, I rolled back on my pillow and fell asleep.

Despite his own sorrow, Luke was endeavoring to surround us with whatever might provide comfort. Each morning, he set out coffee and pastries from the corner bakery and solicitously asked us what we'd like to do. I tried to approximate my old self by suggesting that Luke, Max, Craig, and I—by this time Sam had returned to Seattle to be with his girlfriend, Annie—take the subway to Coney Island for the day. Kelsey adored Coney Island: waves pounding the shore, the scent of salt air mixed with sunscreen, and beachgoers of different sizes, shapes, and colors. I thought Coney Island might lift our spirits. It didn't. We nibbled on hot dogs, ambled along the boardwalk, and gazed at the rides—but we were much more like the flotsam and jetsam on the shore than the lively, laughing holidaymakers we passed by. Luke tried to smile without success, Max fought tears, and Craig hunched over as if trying to protect himself from the consuming pain. I felt as if I'd been thrown off the roller coaster. We got on the elevated train and returned to Luke's apartment, where at least we didn't have to pretend to be having a good time.

That evening, the four of us went to a gathering of Kelsey's family and friends hosted by her friend Ruby and her mom in their Brooklyn home. Ruby, who is Jewish, thought of the get-together as a version of sitting shiva. According to Jewish tradition, shiva refers to the first seven days of mourning after the burial of a loved one. Members of a Jewish community sit shiva by visiting the home of the deceased or their family, bearing food and stories. (Our friend Arthur and his son, Alex, hosted another such gathering for us in Seattle the following week.) Ruby and her mom had prepared most of the food, but each of the guests contributed something. Luke brought a bottle of wine, someone brought bread, someone else brought fruit, and many of the young people shared stories. As I watched Kelsey's friends from college, work, and summer trips, tears clogged my throat. *Damn it, Kelsey,* I thought. *Why aren't you here? You should be eating, talking, and drinking with your friends on a warm, spring night in New York.*

There was no response. Did I think there would be? I wasn't sure, although I was always hopeful. Natalie, Kelsey's roommate from their freshman year in college, sat next to me and said, almost as an aside, "You might not feel Kelsey's presence now because the pain is so great, but as it subsides, you'll feel her with you more and more."

(A few years later—at Katie's wedding—I asked Natalie about that insight, wondering how she'd become so wise at such a young age. She was surprised because she couldn't remember the conversation and didn't recall having had such an astute understanding of the grieving process. Who knows? Maybe Kelsey had responded to me after all—but through Natalie's words.)

After most of the guests had left, Ruby invited Luke, Max, and me to go up to the rooftop. We stepped out of the narrow staircase and onto the deck, all of us relieved, I suspect, that the sadness of the get-together was behind us. I searched for stars but could see only the lights of Brooklyn. In one of the many emails sent to me during the past week, a friend had written that it might help me to imagine Kelsey as now living among the stars. She meant to provide reassurance, but her suggestion made me shudder. I didn't want Kelsey trillions of miles away. I thought of a verse from the Bible: I call heaven and earth to witness against you today that I have set before you life and death, blessings, and curses. Choose life so that you and your descendants may live (Deuteronomy 30:19). The verse seemed to be specifically directed at me: *Don't think so much about Kelsey! Don't keep yearning for a beyond-the-grave relationship with her.*

But then, the earth tilted on its axis As I looked at the stars—or at least where the stars would have been if not for the city lights— Kelsey whispered in my ear, and for once her words felt as real as the sound of a nearby foghorn,

Hey Mom! You are *choosing life. We* are *still connected. We* can *continue our relationship. You'll have to figure out how to do it, but I'll help.*

The stars seemed then like the comforting backing of a quilt and not at all distant.

chapter twelve
Return to Marrowstone

The summer after Sally died, when my cousin Tricia and I were both ten years old, no one said, "Tricia can be your new sister." Still, I had hoped, without saying it aloud, that she would fill the void left by Sally's death. Until that summer, although Tricia was my first cousin, we'd barely spent any time together. She lived in California, and I lived in Illinois. I have pictures that show us together when we were two or three, but I have no memories from that time. I don't know exactly how that summer had been arranged. I imagine Aunt Betty asked my dad how she could help, or maybe my dad approached my aunt. Tricia thinks our grandma planted the idea.

I remember Tricia disembarking the plane after it landed in Chicago. A few curls had escaped from her long braids, her face was both excited and apprehensive, and she was carrying a small bag that I later learned was filled with books. *Will she like me?* I wondered, but deep down I wasn't worried. She was my cousin. We were linked by a family bond. Of course she would like me.

During visits to our grandparents' small town, a forty-five-minute drive from my family's home, the daily routine for Tricia and me included walking to the post office to collect the mail. If it was a Tuesday or a Saturday, we headed upstairs to the library—a large room lined with bookshelves that were filled with many intriguing but often-musty volumes. I will forever associate *Little Women* with that library. The first time I read the novel, it was in an illustrated edition dating to about 1920, plucked from those library shelves. Whenever Tricia and I had a few quarters, the two of us strolled the three blocks from our grandparents' house to Cohen's Groceries, passing by the hog holding shed (which, to our disappointment, was never occupied) and paid for a couple of romance comic books and a box of Betty Crocker vanilla cake mix. As soon as we returned home, we sneaked our purchases to the small, upstairs bedroom in the back of the house and closed the door in order to immerse ourselves in thwarted love affairs while nibbling on clumps of sweet cake mix.

Tricia was unlike me in so many ways. I still occasionally played with dolls, but they held no appeal for her. She was much more interested in the taxidermy she was learning about from an older, second cousin. I had never ventured far from my central Illinois home, but because her dad worked as an efficiency expert for a company with plants in multiple states, Tricia's family moved every two years. The stories she told were magical, transporting me from the monotony of Illinois cornfields and the sadness that was the undercurrent of my family's life to faraway and exotic California. "Tell me more about your friend Sue Lott and your dog Oglethorpe," I begged as we sprawled on the bed. She turned on her side, traced the pattern on the green quilted spread, and launched into another tale.

"Did you think you were sent to save our family?" I asked Tricia a couple of years after Kelsey's death, as we sipped tea next to the fireplace of her Seattle condo—white stucco walls, leaded glass windows, and high wooden beams. She wore a cotton jacket, and her gray hair fell in waves below her ears. Her brown eyes were thoughtful.

"I don't think anyone said that in so many words," she answered, "but I must have believed I was supposed to take care of your family. Sometimes, I got out of bed in the middle of the night to clean your brothers' room, probably because it was the only way I could think of to take care of you."

I laughed. "Well, you know, you really did save us, or at least you saved me."

After Kelsey died, we asked Tricia and Steve—the good-natured and fun-loving man Tricia had met in college and married the year following graduation—to join us on Marrowstone. I wanted to be where our photos, books, and family mementos were, but the sole person on Marrowstone who knew of our loss was our neighbor who was on vacation in Montana. It seemed strange—and immeasurably sad—that this was our home, yet no one had met Kelsey, and no one knew that she had died. For the past twenty-eight years, I'd understood who I was: Kelsey's mom—and then Kelsey, Sam, and Max's mom. But who was I then and there in a place where no one knew anything about my daughter?

Craig and I drove onto the island, slightly ahead of Tricia and Steve, and stopped at the Nordland General Store. I gave my debit card to the cashier to pay for the eggs, milk, and butter in my basket. She looked at the name on the card. "Oh, Barbara," she said, "your neighbor told me about your daughter. I am *so* sorry." My heart exploded with gratitude. Someone on the island understood—an unexpected angel, hanging out at the Nordland General Store.

Once in the house, I unpacked our bags, searching for the treasures I had carried with me from Boston: Kelsey's paisley scarf—which I slept with at night—and the jewelry she'd been wearing when she died: one gold earring and a battered turquoise ring. I couldn't find the ring and grew more panicked with each passing minute. Can't I even hold on to Kelsey's ring? Everyone and everything seemed to be slipping through my fingers. Tricia, Steve, and their small dog, Pippin, arrived while I was searching for the lost ring. Tricia and Steve exchanged looks of alarm, seemingly asking themselves what they'd gotten themselves into. I found the ring at last—nestled at the bottom of my suitcase—and everyone heaved a sigh of relief.

The two of them did their utmost to care for Craig and me: preparing meals, washing dishes, and going on long walks with us. One sunny afternoon, we drove to the nearby state park and wandered along the seaweed-strewn beach. I hadn't been to that beach, and I marveled at its beauty while also thinking about how much Kelsey would have liked it. We plopped ourselves on the sand with our backs pressed against driftwood logs. I fantasized about walking into the waves and never coming back but quickly banished the thought. Although I couldn't imagine what my life without Kelsey would look like, I wanted to live. Steve nudged my arm and pointed to Pippin, nestled next to my leg. Before that afternoon, Pippin hadn't paid the slightest attention to me. "He knows you need comfort," Steve said. I began to cry, overwhelmed by the kindness of a small dog. As we stood to return to the car, Pippin shook himself and trotted off ahead of us, his work done.

That evening, Tricia handed me a book and said, "You told me that the only thing you can read right now is poetry, so I'm giving you this." I rubbed my finger along the cover of *Love Poems from God: Twelve Sacred Voices from the East and West*, translated by Daniel Ladinsky, and flipped to the table of contents. The book was a collection of poetry inspired by twelve long-ago mystics including Saint Francis of Assisi, Rumi, Hafiz, and Saint Teresa of Avila.

"Thank you," I said and gave her a hug. "It looks like what I need."

The next morning, I got up well before everyone else and, still wearing my pajamas, made my way to the couch in the east-facing sitting room. I read through the entire book and then, as dawn light crept into the room, reread the poems that had touched me most deeply. Words and phrases like *soul, forever, infinite, no thought of dying, source of all of us* eased my pain like a soothing balm. I wanted Kelsey to walk through the front door and say, *Hi, Mom, guess you thought I might be gone, but I'm not—I'm still here with you*. That didn't happen, but I could hear her saying, through the poetry: *I have a soul that lasts forever in the infinite source of us all. Give no thought to my dying because dying is not a truth*. I read the entire book again.

When Kelsey was a few weeks old, I spent a morning with Tricia and Steve's two young daughters in their house in Seattle's Capitol Hill—a neighborhood with a plethora of restaurants, coffee shops, and apartment buildings from the 1920s and 30s. Turn-of-the-last-century homes were perched on the top of the hill, and a few elegant estates with views of Elliot Bay and the Cascades were partially visible through tall wrought iron fences on the west-facing side. Every few minutes, Sarah and Christina (six and three years old respectively) interrupted their activities—bouncing on the couch, playing with Legos, chatting with me and their mom—to gingerly extend a finger to Kelsey or stroke her downy cheek. I knew that in a few years, my daughter would be racing through rooms and tumbling on furniture just as her cousins had, but I felt a surge of relief that for the moment she was protected within the radius of my arms—that for at least the next few months, I could shelter her from the dangers that awaited in the world.

I carefully observed Tricia's parenting style, trying to learn from it. She never gave her daughters sugary treats but instead provided them with fresh organic fruits and vegetables. She ensured they had wooden toys that encouraged imagination. She refused to have a TV in the house. But her cautiousness dissipated when it came to their physical safety, or at least that's how it seemed to me. Sarah and Christina climbed to the tops of trees; raced their bikes on cracked, uneven sidewalks; and swam to the middle of the pond outside their summer house—but Tricia didn't so much as flinch while watching them, positive they'd be okay. I was never sanguine about my own kids' safety. Although I tried to mask my fears, I knew, because of my sister, that children could die.

When Kelsey was studying in Ecuador during her junior year of college, I was terrified of accidents, illnesses, and—utterly without a rational basis —the possibility of her being kidnapped by sex traffickers. Craig had to talk me down one night when images of my daughter, bound and gagged, kept me from sleep. Nevertheless, my qualms hadn't prevented her from going back to Ecuador the very next summer or from being part of communities focused on social justice, even if that meant living and working in poor and sometimes dangerous neighborhoods.

Despite my apprehensions, Sam decided to spend a gap year after high school in a Black township outside Stellenbosch, South Africa, living with a township family and working as a teaching assistant at a nearby school. During his own gap year, Max lived with a family in Bolivia, taught the children of prisoners in a Bolivian penitentiary, and rode a bike high in the Bolivian mountains, along North Yungas, which has been described as "the most dangerous road in the world." Living with my children's choices was a tough balancing act. I loved knowing they were experiencing foreign cultures and speaking other languages, but I counted the days—and hours—until they returned home. I rarely worried when I was traveling with the kids, convinced I could keep them safe, but I was on high alert when any one of them was taking a trip on his or her own.

In death, Kelsey was in a place I knew nothing, or next to nothing, about—and she wasn't ever going to return home. How could I reconcile myself to that? Although the book of mystical love poems helped, I longed for Kelsey herself to set my mind at ease. I ached to have a conversation with her.

chapter thirteen

Craig

Each evening after Kelsey's death and our return to Marrowstone, Craig and I sat at the oak table in our dining room, talking about Kelsey and drinking a bottle of wine, never more than one bottle but never less. Fortunately, Craig recognized the peril and one night, without saying a word, corked the bottle after one glass for each of us. I didn't argue. We'd been looking out for each other for the past thirty years of our marriage.

When I was a freshman and Craig was a senior at Carleton College in rural Minnesota our paths *could* have crossed, but they didn't. We knew many of the same people, however, and in the fall of 1968, two years after Craig graduated, one of our mutual friends invited us to dinner at her apartment in Chicago. By that time, Craig was in his second year at Chicago Theological Seminary, and I was a Carleton dropout, taking classes at the University of Illinois in Urbana, 150 miles south of Chicago, and paying off a debt to my dad.

Our mutual friend had been Craig's choreographer for the college musical when he had the lead role: a mime who fears vulnerability and intimacy. I didn't see the show but wish I could go back in time to watch him onstage and hear him sing, "What kind of fool am I," a reflection on never falling in love. The song rang true for Craig in his personal life at the time, and even a decade later, when he and I began dating, I'd been married and divorced twice while he *still* hadn't fallen in love.

I'd heard many things about Craig from Carleton friends, but two things stood out: During his first year at Chicago Theological Seminary, he lived in a seminary-owned house with a Black street gang and was arrested in a police raid of the house. At the time, I didn't have any Black friends, I'd never met a member of a street gang, and I couldn't imagine being arrested.

Craig looked ordinary enough: short brown hair, gray-green eyes, an average height and build. But the smile that lit up his face was anything but ordinary. "I'd love to hear about what you've been doing," I said after our friend introduced us. Craig looked at me and smiled that thousand-watt smile. Emboldened, I continued, "I heard you lived with a Black street gang. And that you were arrested."

His smile was replaced by a more thoughtful expression. "I lived with the Blackstone Rangers for almost a year."

"How did that happen?" I had heard about the Blackstone Rangers as well. Even though what I heard wasn't positive, I was interested in Craig's perspective on what was purported to be a notorious and violent street gang.

He paused, gathering his words. "Some of the faculty thought it would be a good idea for a couple of White students to live in the house with the Rangers. They thought if we lived there, the police might stop raiding, or at least we could be witnesses to the raids. After a couple of months, the other student left, and I was the only non-Ranger in the house."

His words gave me goosebumps. I'd never known anyone who'd done anything remotely similar. "What was it like, living with the Rangers?" I asked.

"It was pretty amazing." Craig's eyes lit up. "I really like the guys. Their leader, Jeff Fort, didn't finish grade school, but I've learned more from him than from all my teachers at college and at the seminary."

I smiled, clearly impressed. "But wasn't it dangerous? Weren't you scared?"

His eyebrows shot up. "Scared of the guys? No. Of the police, yes."

According to friends of mine who'd grown up in Chicago's South Side, members of the gang threatened young kids, requiring them to pay "dues" in exchange for protection. As Craig talked a bit more about the Rangers, I began to see them through his eyes: complicated human beings who sometimes used violence against other gangs but who also responded to racism with a boldness and creativity that led them into direct confrontation with Mayor Richard Daley and the Chicago police.

"During one of many police raids of the house," Craig continued, "the Rangers and I were arrested on a trumped-up charge and taken to an undisclosed location. When I asked to make a phone call, the officer looked at me and stated, 'Where do you think you are? In the United States? Nope, you're in Chicago.'"

I could imagine how scary that must have been. I wanted to wrap my arms around Craig, but I knew that would have been out of place. We'd just met and anyway, I had a boyfriend whom I intended to marry, so I merely said, "That sounds awful. How did you get out?"

"Someone found out about our arrest and told a faculty member. The seminary sent an attorney to post bail—but we had to spend the night behind bars." He shrugged. "We're still waiting for a court date, and it's been months." (Years later, I learned more of the story. The Rangers were beaten while in custody—terrible but not surprising, because that's what the Chicago police seemed to do—and Craig was told they were charging him as an accessory to murder. It took the judge a year to drop the charges.)

He was obviously uncomfortable talking further about the arrest and changed the subject. "What about you? I understand you left college and went to Europe."

I took a deep breath. "I have to begin with last January because that's when the travel agency near campus was promoting student fares to Europe on Icelandic Airlines. Without much thought—probably without *any* thought—I bought a cheap one-way ticket from New York to Luxembourg. It was an open-ended ticket, meaning I could use it at any time. I didn't have specific plans—other than a vague desire to meet up with my boyfriend in Vienna—but that ticket burned a hole in my pocket. A few weeks later, I told my roommate I was leaving school, and asked her to tell everyone else—including my poor parents."

Craig's eyes widened. "How did your parents deal with *that* news?"

"They were frantic. My mom says her hair turned gray because of worrying about me." I tried to smile, but it felt like a thousand pins were pricking my gut.

"They must have been shocked as well as worried: But at least you got to Europe. What'd you do there?"

"That's a long story," I replied, "but the short version is that I traveled for a month with my boyfriend and his friends and then worked for another month in Athens as an au pair. I tried to go to a language school in Paris, but a national strike put the kibosh on that. Because of the strike, the Paris-Metro stopped working and without the metro, I had to walk everywhere. I also joined in some of the nonviolent student protests. After the strike ended, my boyfriend met me in Paris, and we hitchhiked to Yugoslavia, where we spent part of the summer at a Communist youth camp near Zagreb. Then I came home. End of story, except that now I'm living with my parents and working to pay my dad back for the money he lent me so I could come home."

"Phew," Craig said. "You packed a lot into those seven months!"

I nodded. "I'd love to return to Europe if I could afford it. My dad won't pay for me to go back to Carleton, so I'm looking into other schools." I poured Craig a glass of the wine I'd brought to the dinner, and regarded him closely, curious to see how he would react to his fist sip.

"What is *this*?" he asked, puckering. "It tastes like turpentine."

"It's retsina, a Greek wine made from pine resin. You have to develop a taste for it." In truth, my cheap retsina was almost unpalatable, but I liked showing off my newly acquired sophistication. I really hadn't expected Craig to like the wine, but I was gratified he seemed to like *me*. I didn't see him again until seven years later.

When my first marriage—to the boyfriend with whom I'd traveled in Europe—fell apart, I moved to Orcas Island, eighty nautical miles north of Seattle. After visiting me on the island, Tricia and Steve decided to buy a house there along with some acreage. Along the way, I married a good man but with whom I was incompatible in many ways. It was an impulsive marriage, and it wasn't destined to last.

One afternoon in 1975, while on a break from the island and my fraying second marriage, I happened to walk by the clinker-brick Congregational Church in Seattle's Capitol Hill neighborhood. There was Craig's name, in bold letters, on the reader board. My heart leapt. I'd thought about him from time to time during the previous seven years, but the memory of everything he told me about his life in Chicago—along with his warm smile—came rushing back. According to a notice posted on the reader board, he was going to be installed as minister of the church in a special service the next day.

I returned the following afternoon and settled into a pew halfway between the front and back of the church. When Craig, in a black clerical robe, walked up the aisle in a solemn procession with other clergy, he happened to glance at me, and his eyebrows shot up. *He recognizes me!* I felt like dancing in the aisle. In the receiving line that followed the service, he smiled and shook my hand, although he only had time to say "Hello, Barb." *He remembers my name!* That realization felt like starlight in my pocket. I didn't spend much time trying to analyze my feelings, but every time I remembered our brief encounter during the next two years of my ill-fated marriage, my spirits lifted.

After my second divorce, I moved from Orcas Island to an apartment a few blocks from Craig's church. Although I hadn't looked for an apartment near the church, I was glad that's how it worked out. I attended services at the church from time to time, always telling myself that it was because I liked Craig's theology and liturgical style—which was true. He spoke of love rather than sin and of a man named Jesus who radiated compassion rather than judgment. And he was adept at putting together services that had the right timing and lighting and the right mixture of music and words. I didn't admit to an attraction that was more than theological until Christmas loomed, and I joined a group of church members for a caroling party. We had just finished singing "O Come, All Ye Faithful" in front of Craig's apartment building near the church, when he came to the window. I felt a pleasurable tingling up and down my back. But then he was joined by a woman whom I didn't recognize. *Who is she?* I wondered. *And why is she with Craig?* I was surprised by the stabbing sensation in my chest. While drinking hot spiced wine with the other carolers later, I asked, as casually as possible, "Who was that woman with Craig?" Someone said that she was a woman he sometimes dated, but whoever it was didn't think it was serious. Relief flooded through me, and I finally admitted to myself that my attraction to Craig was about more than just theology and liturgy.

When the church offered a series of Lenten vesper services, I attended every one of them. Sometimes, there were only the two of us in the small, candlelit chapel: Craig in front and me in a pew a few rows back. At the end of each service, he offered a blessing, adapted from Numbers 6:24-26 and known as the Priestly Blessing. According to the biblical story, God gave the blessing to Aaron, the brother of Moses, who was a priest. Craig's adaptation retained the power and beauty of the original:

May God bless and keep you.
May God's face shine upon you and be gracious unto you.
May God's countenance be lifted high above you and give
you peace.

Craig's gentle voice felt like a caress. The way his cords fit over his backside made my legs quiver. But I'd fallen in love too easily and too many times, so I wanted to proceed slowly. I attended vesper services and waited to see what might unfold. "Would you like to grab a pizza, or do you have other plans?" Craig asked one night following vespers.

"No, no plans," I answered, although I did have plans to meet friends later for dinner. No matter, I went with him for pizza. A month after that, he asked if I wanted to go canoeing. We paddled his old aluminum canoe into two bays and around two small islands of the Washington Park Arboretum in Seattle. "That's a merganser, and there's a loon," Craig pointed out as we paddled under a bridge and stopped amid the lily pads. A sudden warmth flooded through me. It was strangely sexy that he knew the names of diving ducks. *Yes, let's see where this goes,* I thought—and invited him to have dinner at my apartment the next week. Three years later, we were at last ready to commit to marriage.

Over the years, we've had some difficult moments, most of them because of complex trauma from Craig's early childhood. When triggered by something I've said or done—it might be something as innocuous as me saying it would be nice to get an umbrella for our backyard—Craig has become terrified and retreated to an emotional (and often physical) space that seemed safer. In the early years of our marriage, finding a safe space meant he abruptly stopped talking, went to bed, and stayed under the covers, not looking at me or saying a word, for as long as a day or two. To me, it was a sudden and inexplicable abandonment. I often made matters worse through my tearful, enraged questions (sometimes accompanied by stomping my foot or slamming my fist on the kitchen counter): "What is *happening*?" "What have I *done*?" "Why are you *doing* this to me?" Over the years, as Craig learned more about his trauma and engaged with therapy, the episodes became shorter and occurred far less often. And, as I understood more about the reasons for his withdrawals and also undertook therapy, I got better at weathering them, no longer quite so bewildered and angry. The episodes have become less frequent and the very few that do occur are not long-lasting. Our individual psychological issues—trauma for Craig and a sense of abandonment for me—are firestorms that could have destroyed our relationship. That they didn't is due to our deep caring for each other—and to the help of skilled therapists.

Because of his trauma, Craig was self-protective and, at times, emotionally distant from me and the kids. A few days after Dad's memorial service, Kelsey called him on his cell phone. I couldn't hear what she was saying, but I saw Craig's eyes widen and watched as his fists clenched and unclenched. Afterward, he told me that Kelsey was hurt he hadn't called in the days following her grandfather's death. When he said to her that it had been hard to find the time to call, she countered with the statement, "Dad, you can always find the time to call."

That was their last conversation, and I was worried. *Will Craig always feel regret?* But in fact, he took her words as an invitation and found time to *call* her—during moments of sitting quietly at home, on walks, and later during silent worship at our Quaker meeting. And he found time not only to call but also to *hold* Sam, Max, and me as we wept. He let us know that he was always available, whenever and wherever we needed him.

The boxes containing Kelsey's belongings—sweaters, shoes, dresses, books, and journals—arrived at the post office a couple of miles south of our Seattle apartment. Craig and I lifted each of the heavy boxes into the back of our Subaru and unloaded them in the garage of our apartment building. After two more trips to the post office, we piled the boxes onto two dented grocery carts, pushed the carts into the elevator, and then down the long corridor to our apartment. Craig's bowed head and stooped back made me sad beyond words. The piled boxes sat in our bedroom closet for several days. We knew we needed to sort through them, so one rainy afternoon a few friends showed up to help. Kelsey's belongings brought her back so vividly that, for a split second, it seemed like she was alive—until the terrible realization that she was dead left me reeling in pain.

Without wine to get us through the evenings, we began going to bed early. One night, I was transported in my sleep to a waterfall that flowed into a series of pools, reminiscent of the mountain pools of Priest Lake. Gentle life-giving water washed over me for what seemed like hours. I awakened, still sad but feeling like I'd been accompanied through the night by Kelsey. On other nights, one of the Hebrew prayers that Pam had texted me after Kelsey's death played in my head straight through to morning:

May the source of strength,
who blessed the ones before us,
help us find the courage to
make our lives a blessing.

Whenever I awoke in the middle of the night, aching with loss, I left the bed, trying not to disturb Craig. I stumbled across the room to the open window and waited for the resident barred owls. I was rarely disappointed. Their syncopated calls felt like messages from the world beyond.

At some point during that summer, Craig asked if I was interested in making love. "I don't know," I said, "maybe." I *was* interested, but the trouble was, I didn't know where Kelsey was. *Maybe she can see everything we do. Maybe she's in the room with us.* It didn't seem right to have sex in front of our daughter.

Then I remembered a time, several years before, when Craig and I were traveling in Germany. The day had been so hot and humid that we decided against taking a walk and went instead to our hotel room to cool off. We'd just settled in, each of us with a book, when a breeze fluttered the curtains and the room filled with the slightly metallic air of an approaching thunderstorm. We walked over to the windows and gazed at the fields of sunflowers and wheat just beyond the hotel and at the gathering storm clouds in the distance. The sky darkened. A few drops began to fall, a slow waltz that quickly built to a crescendo. Streaks of lightening lit the fields, thunder rolled, and the sweet scent of clean earth filled the room. We touched lightly, first fingers and palms, then wrists, then necks, slowly exploring, kindling desire.

The memory brought back the sensation of being a part of everything around me. Maybe I could open myself to sorrow, confusion, and uncertainty and still find pleasure in making love to someone I truly and deeply loved.

chapter fourteen
Kelsey's Memorial Service

"I've lost my leader," Sam said. He straightened his shoulders and looked directly at the family and friends gathered in the pews in front of him. He was accustomed to giving sermons—he'd just finished seminary with a year-long internship at a church in Berkeley—but speaking at his sister's memorial service, saying some of what was in his broken heart, was much harder. He had indeed lost his leader. He finished his comments by paraphrasing Psalm 19:

> *The heavens are telling of her glory and the firmament proclaims her handiwork.*
> *Day to day pours forth speech, and night to night declares knowledge.*
> *There is no speech, nor are there words; her voice is not heard,*
> *Yet her voice goes out through all the earth and her words to the end of the world.*

I wanted to write that "Yet" on my heart because it defied doubt, it was a word that proclaimed the inexplicable veracity of spirit. I needed its power and fortitude, especially during my daughter's memorial service.

Craig and I had penned a short obituary for Kelsey because we couldn't stand the concept of *obituary* for our vibrant, life-loving daughter. David Paul, a dear friend and also Kelsey's godfather, submitted it to the newspaper: "Our beloved Kelsey died on June 1 in a bike/bus accident in Boston. We are heartbroken, and we are grateful for twenty-eight joy-filled years with her. A memorial service will be held on Saturday, June 23, 2:00 p.m. at Plymouth Congregational Church in Seattle."

Sam drove Craig, Max, and me to the downtown church where we had decided to hold the service to accommodate the many expected attendees. I got out of the car and walked from the parking garage toward the church with my husband and sons but, as was so painfully obvious, without my daughter.

The minister ushered us into a side room. "Your family can wait in here until just before the service begins," he said. Soon, more than fifty family members—our parents, sisters, brothers, sisters- and brothers-in-law, nieces, nephews, and cousins—filled the room. No one said a word other than "Hello" for thirty minutes. If Craig and I had been able to speak, the others would have followed, but we were too grief-stricken. The minister apologized later, "I thought you'd be more comfortable together in a room rather than in the sanctuary. I had no idea you wouldn't talk." But we wouldn't have been comfortable anywhere.

One of the hymns we had chosen was Duke Ellington's "Come Sunday," which includes the words, *"God of love."* In the days before the service, I worried that the hymn was too religious for Kelsey and, since I wasn't on very good terms with God, even too religious for me. The night before the service, I had this dream: *In the mistiness of the world to come, Kelsey gestures toward an elderly Black man wearing red suspenders who is walking by, just a few yards behind her. She says to me, "That's Duke Ellington, Mom. If you want to include his song in the service, it's fine with me."* After the dream, I stopped being concerned about using the hymn and developed a soft spot for Duke Ellington with his—at least in my mind—fondness for red suspenders.

A few rays of sun filtered through the stained glass windows. I turned to look at those who had gathered in the sanctuary. Our family members filled the first four rows. Behind them I could distinguish a few familiar faces, the rest were a blur. I felt lightheaded. *This just can't be real,* I thought. After Sam finished his comments, he removed his notes from the lectern and joined Craig, Max, and me in the front pew.

When packing up Kelsey's papers and books in her Boston apartment a few weeks earlier, Max had found a Spanish translation of a scriptural passage. He read the passage at the service, first in English: "Love is patient; love is kind; love is not envious or boastful or arrogant or rude. It does not insist on its own way; it is not irritable; it keeps no record of wrongs." (1Corinthians 13:4-5). Then in Spanish, using the translation he'd found amid Kelsey's papers.

Ever since the piano prelude, I'd been listening for Kelsey's voice. I thought maybe I could detect something, but it was impossible to know. As Max finished his reading, I finally could hear her: *Yes, love is patient and kind, but love also laughs! I know you're sadder than you've ever been, Mom, but I think you'll find me in laughter.*

Kelsey's cousin Benj may have picked up on that because he talked about a time when Kelsey wanted to dress up as a stop sign for Halloween. She couldn't figure out how to construct the costume, so she asked Benj for help. The finished costume was so cumbersome that she had to walk sideways when Trick-or-treating with her friends, but that didn't bother her. The next year she dressed up as a picnic table.

See? Doesn't it help to laugh, Mom?

Our adventure-loving niece Melissa recounted a story from a couple of years before when she and Kelsey traveled by camel through an Indian desert. Kelsey engaged in a long conversation with their guide, asking questions about his life. "Listening to their give-and-take was definitely the best part of the trip," Melissa said.

Another of Kelsey's cousins, Zac, said that in his work as a public defender, he often thought of Kelsey and her devotion to social justice. His words reminded me of a time when Kelsey was a preschooler. Zac, who was a few years older and far more versed in biology, told her, "You're an animal."

Three-year-old Kelsey was outraged. "I am *not* an animal!" Nothing Zac said could convince her otherwise. She knew when something didn't feel right.

Our niece Brynn, a first-grade teacher, talked about how much the three kids in her family and the three kids in ours hated to say goodbye after holiday visits. To counter their sadness, they gathered and hid on the floor of the departing car, hoping no one would notice. Brynn was feeling now a similar but much deeper sorrow at having to say goodbye to Kelsey.

I thought about those holiday visits. For every Thanksgiving, our family of five drove down to my brother's house in Portland, and my parents, along with my other brother and his family—all of them living in California—met us there. The kids grew close during those Thanksgiving get-togethers and while attending our annual reunions at a conference center on Monterey Bay in California. They grew even closer on subsequent, longer family trips to the Midwest, the East Coast, and Europe.

Shortly before the memorial service, Brynn and Melissa gave me a necklace with a tiny shamrock—Kelsey was born on Saint Patrick's Day—and said that Kelsey was more like their sister than their cousin. As they talked about Kelsey during the service, I fingered the necklace, now around my neck.

Hey, Mom, why don't you think about how much you love Brynn and Melissa? That'll help.

Kelsey's friends from the neighborhood in which she had grown up spoke next. They used to imagine they were adults, doing all kinds of grown-up things—making films, writing books, getting married, having kids—but they never imagined dying. I hoped they could use their imaginations to make sense of her death, hoped they could feel what I was beginning to trust—at least some of the time and certainly during her memorial service—that she was still with us.

As one person after another spoke about Kelsey, memories of her coursed through my head: her smile, her eyes, her heart-shaped birthmark, her beautiful curly brown hair. When she was just two years old, I cut her hair short in a kind of pixie cut, thinking it would revive the curls she'd had as a baby. It didn't, and she hated having short hair, even at age two. From then on, she let her hair grow, wearing it in braids or a long ponytail, until right before she started high school when she had it cut to her shoulders. Her shorter hair waved in irrepressible curls. "Oh, Mom, I hate my hair!" she'd cried.

"Kelsey, it looks beautiful. Why don't you like it?"

"I don't look like myself." She gathered her hair and pulled it into a tight ponytail.

"Why are you doing that?" I asked in dismay. "Your curls are lovely."

She shrugged and tugged the ponytail even tighter. Throughout the rest of her life, she never liked her haircuts. They were never quite right and never matched what she'd imagined. And I always wanted her to stop defaulting to ponytails.

When she was in middle school, I took her clothes shopping. She was at an in-between stage, no longer a child but not yet an adult, and was developing curvy hips and breasts. We had a hard time finding clothes that both fit and appealed to an adolescent. Until then, Kelsey had looked like me—we even wore the same shoe size—but her body had begun to grow in a voluptuous way that was a mystery to me. I chided her whenever she ate pasta Alfredo, which she adored, and urged her to "eat more healthfully." She knew I really meant, *Don't eat foods that add to your curves.*

Kelsey's Boston friend Ginny told me that Kelsey was a different person when speaking Spanish or dancing at a Dominican bar—more sensual and open. I loved imagining my gorgeous, curvy daughter, swaying to the music, laughing, flirting, flicking her hair out of her eyes, and completely at home in her body.

Kelsey had gone on dates with people she'd met in person and online and was frustrated that a special man hadn't yet made an appearance in her life. I found myself spending a lot of time worrying and even praying about her finding a mate. If I could change the past, I'd sympathize with her frustration, but I would know, in both heart and head, that she was perfect as she was—with or without a partner. If I could change the past, I would smile in delight at her ponytail and offer her more pasta.

The three kids and I developed a ritual of going clothes shopping the day after Christmas. I remember a lunch at the Italian restaurant on the first level of Westlake Center in downtown Seattle. We found a table toward the back of the restaurant and piled our winter coats and bags on an empty chair. Reaching for the menu, I asked the kids, "Did you get everything you wanted, or do you have more shopping to do?"

Max nodded. "I think I'm finished with my shopping."

"I still haven't found any pants I like," Kelsey said, looking up from her menu.

"Kelsey! It always takes you ten times as long as Max and me to find clothes you like," Sam complained between bites of a breadstick while trying to decide whether he could eat one or two entrées to fill his growing, football-playing body.

"I know the pants I want, and I haven't found them yet," replied Kelsey.

"What do you want?" I asked, suddenly curious. "Have you seen something you like?"

"No, not really, but I know what I want them to look like: low-rise with a pocket on the side and in a soft gray. And I want buttons, not a zipper."

Sam grimaced, "There probably isn't a pair of pants like that in the entire state."

I treasured those lunches, especially after the kids left for college—the three of them all in one place, close to me, chatting about their lives and teasing one another. Over the years, Kelsey never ceased having an exact image in her mind of what she wanted to buy, informed by who knows what. It wasn't at all unusual for her to look for weeks before purchasing a pair of pants or a summer dress.

I knew that she liked dangly earrings, so on a trip to Mexico with a friend, I bought her a pair. I'm not sure where I was at the time, but the handmade jewelry in the shop was exquisite. I have a clear memory of holding a pair of hammered gold earrings in my hand and feeling a frisson of delight. They were perfect for Kelsey.

That's the way it was, again and again. Kelsey gave me such happiness, even when she was thousands of miles away from me, even when I couldn't hear her voice. She was wearing those long gold earrings when she died. That made me feel a tiny bit better. A part of me had been with her.

chapter fifteen
Dreams and Reassurances

I suddenly hear a telephone ringing. Images of my extended family swirl around and around until finally coming to a halt. All of us are eager to learn who is calling. We discover that it's Kelsey. She lets us know—completely without words—that she is fine: stronger and more truly herself than we could ever imagine. I know—and my whole family knows—that the call changes everything.

I had the dream in the early morning hours following Kelsey's service. It was hazy, a swirling cloud, and it echoed part of Psalm 19 which Sam had paraphrased at the memorial service:

> *There is no speech, nor are there words; her voice is not heard,*
> *Yet her voice goes out through all the earth and her words to*
> *the end of the world.*

I felt light, as if I were floating. I wanted to shout to the rooftops, "Kelsey is fine!" *That's all I need*, I told myself. *There is nothing to be sad about.* But of course, there was. This blissfulness lasted for a couple of hours, replaced by all-too-familiar, heart-stopping pain.

Nevertheless, the dream was important. It lived in the deepest part of me. I *knew* Kelsey was fine. I *knew* she was stronger and more herself than I could ever imagine. But, while that was true, something else was true as well: I still had doubts, still felt hopeless, still despaired.

In the weeks after the service, I got up each morning, lured by the promise of strong coffee, but moving an arm or a leg seemed to take an extraordinary amount of energy. When I tried to do paperwork, I shuffled between the study and the dining room, barely able to lift my feet. When Craig and I went shopping, I tried to act like a normal person, but I felt like a fraud. I wanted to shout out to everyone who passed by, "My daughter is dead!"

I thought often of Meursault, the main character in Albert Camus's book *The Stranger*. Like Meursault in the heat of the Algerian desert, I felt a sense of nothingness. As soon as we returned from shopping, I grabbed a book, usually one about grief, attempting to fill the void, hungry to find reassurance that Kelsey still existed. A part of me continued to agonize about the moments preceding Kelsey's death. *Did she know the bus was coming? Was she terrified?*

In *Polishing the Mirror: How to Live from Your Spiritual Heart*, Ram Dass compares dying to "taking off a tight shoe." That soothed me. My friend Pam, who often texted me poems and songs, sent me a book by Andrew Barone and George Anderson, *Walking in the Garden of Souls*. Although I was taken aback by the book which seemed to veer from Pam's usual taste—it had been recommended to her by another grieving friend—I read it from cover to cover. Anderson, a medium, claims that souls in the world beyond have told him that any suffering associated with dying is erased the moment one steps out of this world and into the next. I wasn't completely convinced of Anderson's authenticity, but *that* message I chose to believe.

In the middle of the summer, before a planned visit from Sam and Annie, I decided to load our cookie jar with chocolate-chip cookies to let Sam know that we were ready to stand on our own, that he didn't need to worry about us, that he could get on with his own life and his own grieving. It was so damned hard to make those cookies! The measuring spoons were too heavy to lift, the stirring took an inordinate amount of energy, and I constantly had to repeat steps. But it was worth the effort. Sam walked into our house and went straight to the cookie jar. "Mom, you made cookies!" he exclaimed, a big smile on his face. Love—and a wave of relief—washed over me along with the realization: *I can still take care of* this *child.*

It was challenging to parent our grieving children—even to know how to begin. Sam came to Marrowstone by himself and spent time walking through the woods and along the beaches. One day he asked, "Can you come with me to the beach, Mom? I want to go swimming, but I don't know how my body will react to the cold." I stood on the windy shore, watching as he swam back and forth in the fifty-degree water without a wetsuit. He emerged with a huge grin, eager to wrap himself in a warm towel. I thought of his swimming as an act of purification, a shedding of his former life and a turning toward new wholeness. But the actual words he used were, "That felt just right."

After being in Seattle to attend Kelsey's memorial service a few days following his twenty-first birthday, Max flew to New York for a summer internship that involved providing food and companionship to youths living on the street. He stayed in his cousin Luke's Brooklyn apartment. Because each of them knew the other was grieving, they didn't have to explain or make excuses for the times when sadness overwhelmed either or both of them.

Craig and I called Max every day or two to check in, and he came to Seattle at the end of his internship to spend a week with us before returning to Swarthmore for his senior year. I wanted to find words to ease his pain, but—as I should have known—there were no such words. The best I could do was to wait for the moments when he was ready to talk and then just listen.

It was hard for Max to be back in school because few of his friends understood the depth of his unhappiness. He broke up with his girlfriend, in large part because she wondered why he couldn't move on. (After her dad died unexpectedly a year later, she called him to say she then understood.) He met another student, whose mother had died about the same time as Kelsey, and they were able to support each other. He immersed himself in his work for a professor who was renowned—especially in the Quaker world of which Swarthmore was a part—for promoting nonviolent ways of resolving conflicts. And he began to consider taking a cross-country bike trip after he finished his post-graduate premed courses. He thought it would help him come to peace with Kelsey's death. I understood, but thinking of him biking across country unnerved me.

I thought about our three kids all the time, just as I had done through the years, keeping an account of sorts in my head: *How are they doing? What do they need? How can I help?* Although I worried about them, Sam and Max seemed to be learning how to survive the upheaval of Kelsey's death. But I had so many questions about Kelsey beyond *Where is she?* which, at last, was losing its hold on me. I wanted to know if there was anything she needed, if there was any way I could help, and, most troubling of all, if I was holding her back because of my grieving (as one of my Buddhist-leaning friends had suggested). There seemed to be no way to find the answers, short of a conversation with Kelsey.

Hi sweetie, I'm worried that my aching heart is preventing you from moving along in your own journey. Is that right? Am I holding you back?

Her response came in the guise of a dream: *Kelsey is standing next to a track at a train station. She tells me, "I'm waiting for your train to come in. I'll be with you until it does."* It seemed that I could let the grieving unfold naturally without being concerned about preventing Kelsey from her own afterlife journey.

chapter sixteen
Canoe Journey

The tiny dots on the horizon swelled until, finally, I could distinguish them as canoes with jutting prows. In another minute, I could see the gleam of paddles dipping into and out of the water and detect a rhythmic chanting, faint at first but becoming clearer, in sync with the paddles. The foremost canoe—carved out of a single cedar log and painted with traditional Northwest Coast Indian designs—approached the shore of Fort Worden State Park in Port Townsend, Washington. Once it had arrived in the shoals, the paddles were stilled, and the skipper took hold of a megaphone, which had been passed to him by someone on the beach. After telling the name and the home of his tribe, he stated that the crew was tired and hungry and requested permission to come ashore. A member of the local S'Klallam tribe welcomed them in both English and Klallam and then issued an invitation for that evening: "We have food and stories for you and drumming and singing for after the meal." Several men and women, wearing Native garb, pulled the canoe to the shore, accompanied by drumming from farther up the beach.

About fifty canoes, each with twenty to forty pullers and a skipper, had set out early in the morning from the Jamestown S'Klallam landing, about seventeen nautical miles to the west. The crews, along with their families and friends, would spend the night at the Jefferson County Fairgrounds and leave early the next morning for Port Gamble, another seventeen nautical miles to the southeast. Their final destination was the traditional Squaxin landing in Olympia—seventy-five nautical miles south—where they would be joined by an additional fifty canoes coming from as far away as northern California and British Columbia. Approximately ten thousand people in all would spend a week on the Squaxin reservation, eating, dancing, singing, and sharing stories.

The twenty-fourth annual Pacific Northwest Canoe Journey was taking place during the summer immediately following Kelsey's death. Craig and I walked among the canoes, occasionally reaching out to place a finger on a thwart or stroke a cedar bow. Although I later learned we really weren't supposed to touch the canoes, I felt a tingling up and down my arms and a growing lightness in my chest when I did so. Spirit seemed to be all around, in everyone and everything. I filled my lungs with the briny air and slowly released my breath. *If only I could stay here forever,* I thought. But I couldn't. I was only borrowing spiritual awareness from the pullers and the skippers, from the drummers and the greeters, finding hope through *their* spiritual practices and beliefs. The sense of buoyancy began to dissipate, replaced by what had become my habitual melancholy.

Did I ever have the certainty that all was Spirit, that there was no division between this world and the next? Did I ever have an awareness that transcended the ordinary world? I tried to remember. *Maybe.* I remembered past moments of liminality: a deep inner peace while sitting next to a river when I was about eleven years old; feeling at one with the night while parked on a country road the summer following my graduation from high school; a sense of knowing I was where I was meant to be while taking off in a plane bound for Europe, having just left Carleton with little money and no idea of what I'd do once I arrived.

And then there was one very strange olfactory experience. When Max was in high school, he and I were in the car, on our way to do some kind of errand or another, a few months after the death of our sixteen-year-old dog, Sarey. All at once the car was suffused with a familiar and not very pleasant scent: the acrid odor of Sarey's skin caused by a medical condition. "Sarey?" Max asked, his eyes wide.

I nodded. We both laughed but were at a loss to understand what had happened. Had the odor been hidden in the upholstery for the past several months, or had Sarey greeted us from the next world?

Over the years, I'd made many decisions based on intuition. When I was finishing my PhD, rather than pursuing an academic position, I decided to join a small group of people who were working to start a social services and educational agency for homeless families, certain it was what I should do. At another point in my life, following a presentation by incarcerated students in a prison-based university, I approached the program's director and volunteered to teach a class about the psychology of trauma. I had a visceral certitude about doing so.

My intuition was especially strong when making decisions about where to live. Although I grew up in the Midwest and attended school on the East Coast, I felt irresistibly drawn to the Pacific Northwest. When seeing for the first time each of the houses Craig and I bought over the years of our marriage, I felt, within seconds, an intuitive gut punch that told me: *This is the one.*

I had always been able to decipher other people's feelings with some ease, relying not only on physical cues, such as facial expressions or tone of voice, but also on energy vibrations. After Kelsey's death, I wondered whether, by softening my gaze and listening more intently, I could pick up *otherworldly* vibrations. Could I use whatever intuition I had developed over the years to see what was hidden?

The trouble was that Kelsey's death made me doubt my previous hunches and intuitive experiences. *Maybe*, I thought, *there is nothing other than what is right before my eyes, nothing other than what I can rationally explain.* I couldn't seem to move beyond a place of doubt.

chapter seventeen
Dobie Tom

The shaman didn't dispel the pain Craig and I shared, but he did set us on the path toward healing. About a month after Kelsey's death, we met with Dobie Tom at the Catholic church on the Swinomish Reservation, less than an hour from his Lummi home and a little over two hours (including a ferry ride) from our home on Marrowstone. The church, white with a tall steeple, overlooks the Swinomish Slough that separates the reservation from the town of La Conner.

My cousin Tricia met us at the door and introduced us to Father Tuohey. "Welcome," he said, extending his hand. His eyes were kind behind glasses that had slipped toward the tip of his nose. He had traveled two hours from Seattle to open the church for us. Although he was no longer the priest of the church, he spoke Lushootseed and had close, continuing friendships with many Native people in the area.

A dented car, streaked with rust, sputtered into the lot, and Dobie Tom—deep lines etching his face and his white hair pulled into a long, low ponytail—unfolded his legs and climbed out. His son, middle-aged, with acne scars across his cheeks, reached into the back seat to pull out a large drum. "Good, we're all here," Father Tuohey said. "Let's go inside."

He walked ahead of us into a large, sun-filled room lined with bleachers. Several folding chairs were set up on the floor. "This is our Indian sanctuary. There's a traditional sanctuary on the other side," he explained. "Sit wherever you feel comfortable." He then climbed halfway up the bleachers to join Dobie's son, while the rest of us settled on the folding chairs. Dobie pushed his chair around until he faced us. My heart pounded. I was ready to follow him even though I didn't know where we were going.

A couple of weeks before, I'd been in an art gallery, not far from Marrowstone. The back room of the Jamestown S'Klallam Art Gallery was filled with handcrafted wooden furniture, brightly painted Native masks, large wooden rattles, and Northwest Coast–style carvings of eagles, ravens, and hummingbirds. The front room, sunlight streaming in through the windows, was chock-a-block with books, calendars, knickknacks, and CDs. I stopped in front of the CD rack to study a photo of a Native drummer. All at once, I broke into a sweat, and my breath grew ragged. *I need a Native healing,* I thought. My yearning was as strong as a current at peak tide and almost forced me to my knees. It was all I could do to keep from asking the S'Klallam woman behind the counter if she could point the way. A few days later, I asked Tricia if she knew of a shamanic healer through her work with the Chief Seattle Club—a nonprofit agency dedicated to "physically and spiritually supporting American Indian and Alaska Native people." She did—and made the connection.

"I'll tell you a story," Dobie said as he sat close to us in the Native sanctuary. "I was asked to help a man who'd had two heart attacks. The man recovered in body but not in spirit, so his wife asked me for assistance. I journeyed into the next world to see what was happening and found the man's soul at the Gates of Heaven. He couldn't get into Heaven—not yet. It wasn't his time. I returned his soul to him, and he got better. I'm going to journey to Heaven now and see how I can help the two of you."

Dobie's son began drumming, a steady pounding of drum beater on drum. A few seconds later, Dobie started to chant, his voice at first raspy and halting but gradually gaining strength until the entire space resonated with heart-piercing notes, like the song of an orca. I closed my eyes, unable to tell the difference between the beating of my heart and the drum. Slowly, my neck and shoulders relaxed. *I don't want this to end*, I thought as tears rolled down my face. When the chanting stopped in twenty minutes, maybe an hour—the notion of *time* had ceased—I opened my eyes, loath to return to ordinary life. Tricia, also in tears, handed me a tissue.

"I traveled to Heaven and found Kelsey," said Dobie. "She's good." He paused and then explained his spiritual beliefs. "I think all of us have two spirits. One spirit gives us guidance in this life, and the other spirit is what lives on in Heaven after we die. Your guiding spirits were lost, and so I brought them back to you." He studied us for several seconds. "You look better," he said softly. "Now you'll have guidance through your pain." He had additional words for me: "You have to let her go." Even though I'd struggled with the concept of letting go, I knew what he meant. He'd seen my spirit hammering at the Gates of Heaven, pleading to be admitted, begging for a glimpse of Kelsey. But it wasn't my time.

"I've brought something for lunch," Tricia announced, her eyes resting for a moment on Dobie. "I hope you and your son will join us. I've set it up in the kitchen." We walked down the hallway to the kitchen and sat around the vinyl-covered table. Craig and I were silent, absorbed in our own thoughts, while the others chatted quietly. Tricia drew a blue-and-white handmade quilt from her bag and handed it to Dobie. "I know you don't take money for healings, but we want to give you this quilt. It's an old one from our family."

"Thank you," said Dobie folding the quilt and setting it next to the drum. He looked at Craig and then at me, murmuring softly, "Losing a child is especially hard. I'll be in touch."

"How was it for you?" I asked Craig as soon as we got in the car and started out of the parking lot. I was curious to hear what he thought since he had agreed to accompany me only after learning both Tricia and a priest would be present and that the healing would take place in a church.

A smile spread slowly across his face. "It was wonderful," he said, his eyes sparkling. "I traveled with Dobie to Heaven and saw Kels in the middle of a long flowing stream of people going back millennia, a river of wise people." He paused for a while, lost in the memory, and then, still smiling, asked, "What about you?"

"I cried the whole time," I replied. I reflected on my experience for a while and then added, "I didn't see Kelsey, but I feel better. More hopeful."

Northwest Coast tribal families, like those on the Swinomish Reservation or on the Lummi Reservation where Dobie Tom lived, meet every few years for a potlatch—days of feasting, dancing, singing, and gift giving. The potlatch is a time to bestow not only material goods such as blankets and utensils but also the rights to family names, stories, and songs—the right to a song probably the most valued gift of all. At Kelsey's memorial service, we sang a song from her favorite movie *Crooklyn* directed by Spike Lee. Our irrepressible nephew Nathan spontaneously stood up at the opening bars and faced the congregation to lead us in singing "O-o-h Child."

Now that we had our guiding spirits back with us, I realized that the song—and Nathan's impromptu decision to lead it—was a gift, a promise. One day things would get easier, one day life would get brighter.

chapter eighteen
Grieving as a
Spiritual Practice

"You know," said my friend Judith, as we sat in a small park over-looking Lake Washington with the Cascade Mountains looming in the distance, "I think grieving could be a spiritual practice." She ran her fingers through her long, light brown hair, leaned her back against the park bench, and turned toward me, her eyes questioning, "What do you think?"

I sucked in my breath. It was a novel idea. Nothing I'd read in the many books on grief stacked next to my bed and nothing friends or family members had said to me in the six weeks since my daughter had died even suggested that this godawful pain *could* become part of a spiritual practice. Before Kelsey's death, Judith and I had talked—on the patio of her brightly painted house in San Miguel de Allende, Mexico, or on walks near her Seattle apartment in the Capitol Hill neighborhood—about the transformative power of her own spiritual practice. Judith was part of a Buddhist Sangha, and her practice included daily meditation. Her spiritual routine was central to her life and kept her grounded despite living half of the year in Mexico and the other half in Seattle. She also practiced *metta* by blessing herself and moving on to bless all sentient beings, thus spreading kindness and well-being throughout the entire planet.

"Maybe you're right," I said, with hope, like a fleeting image, beginning to gain substance.

The year before Kelsey died, I'd experienced a kind of spiritual awakening. On a flight home from Philadelphia—where I'd led a three-day training session on emotional trauma and then attended a workshop on Quaker simplicity—I became engrossed in a book I'd purchased at the workshop: *A Testament of Devotion* by Thomas R.

Kelly, an early-twentieth-century Quaker teacher and writer. Kelly writes of learning to live life on two levels: on the more superficial level, one goes about the tasks of ordinary life—working, eating, meeting with friends—while on the deeper level, one prays without ceasing. Eventually, the prayer becomes wordless, more of an openness to Spirit and to spiritual guidance. Our life becomes an act of prayer. Throughout the entire cross-country flight, I read the book and prayed as Kelly advised, just below the surface: while eating the meal served by a harried flight attendant, while adjusting my seat and tightening my seatbelt, while looking out the window at the bright blue sky and trailing clouds.

Back at home, early the next morning, I had a vivid, half-awake kind of dream in which the sky parted to reveal a sacred truth. I exclaimed to Craig, "None of this is important!" He nodded. I loved it that he understood even though I hadn't been explicit. Although I had no words for what was revealed or even a clear memory of it, I realized that the activities that dominated my life—leading workshops on trauma, working as a consultant with the public schools, planning a vacation, finishing a kitchen remodel—were peripheral to what was most important. I didn't know how to articulate what *was* important, but the realization that I was missing something fundamental at the heart of existence caused me to yearn for a more spiritual life. While I was pondering where to begin, I had a phone conversation with Kelsey who was, at the time, teaching school in East Harlem.

"How was your workshop on simplicity, Mom?" she asked.

"It was fabulous, and as a result I'm trying to figure out how to simplify my life. I can't really give up work, but I'd like to do something to streamline things at home."

"Like what for instance?"

"Oh, I suppose I should do something about the boxes of saved photos. I rarely look at them, so maybe I should just throw them away."

"No, no, no! Don't throw them away! I want to look through them before you do anything. But, if not the photos, what else can you do?

"I suppose I could clean closets. They're a mess."

"Sure, why not?"

Cleaning closets may not seem particularly spiritual, but trust me, it was. My life had too much clutter, manifested by our overflowing closets. Over the summer, I tackled my bedroom closet, the linen closet, and the kitchen pantry. The effort and especially the result felt good. *Those Quakers were on to something*, I thought. Then I began addressing other aspects of my life. A friend and I held a silent worship service at our church before the regularly scheduled Sunday service. Four or five of us gathered in the parlor next to the pastor's office and sat for thirty to forty minutes without saying a word; afterward, we shared with one another what we had sensed in the silence. I felt increasingly connected to God, although less and less able to articulate what I meant by *God*. I began skipping the regular service; the clatter of spoken prayers and a twenty-minute sermon—even one delivered by my beloved husband—grated on my ears. I craved silence.

Judith's suggestion, that grief could be a spiritual practice, was like a continuation of Thomas Kelly's invitation to pray without ceasing. I grieved without ceasing; perhaps my pain could be turned into prayer—not the "Our Father" or the "Now I lay me down to sleep kind," but something entirely different, an openness to Spirit rather than a prayer with words. A spiritual practice seemed like a way to ease the anguish of loss or at least to give it shape and purpose.

I thought I'd start with meditating, using my breath for guidance. I'd meditated in the past but never for more than a few minutes and never regularly. Ready to make a start, I slipped out of bed soon after sunrise on Marrowstone Island, brushed my teeth—it struck me as strange that the mundane activities of life continued even though the core of my life had fallen apart—and went downstairs to grind beans for the French press. I covered the pot with a thick cozy to keep the coffee hot. I didn't know exactly what I'd do, but the promise of hot coffee at the end was motivating. I settled on one end of the living room sofa, crossed my legs with my feet tucked under my knees, and peered through the French doors, searching for my special leaf. Every morning for the past several weeks, one solitary maple leaf at the bottom of the hill had waved to me. I saw the waving leaf as a lighthearted greeting from Kelsey, equivalent to the "Hi, Mom!" that used to begin our phone conversations.

I closed my eyes, set the intention to be open to Kelsey, wherever she was, and slowly inhaled, paying attention only to my breath, sinking deeper and deeper into an inner space. After some time, images began to appear. Like I was watching a movie, I saw myself in the car, hearing the phone ring, wondering who might be calling, then answering and hearing the awful news about Kelsey's death; I saw myself walking into Craig's and my Seattle apartment and hugging Sam, then going to bed and sobbing. Everything surrounding her death that had become a blur—the trip to Boston, holding her ashes, traveling to New York, visiting her friends—came sharply into focus. Images poured into my head and heart for a solid two hours, and throughout the entire time, I wept. When the meditation ended, I felt better. I didn't know why it was important to relive those moments; it happened naturally. (I recently read "A Meditation on Grief" by Buddhist writer and wisdom teacher Jack Kornfield, published on the website, *Grateful Living.*[1] One might meditate on grief, Kornfield suggests, by letting the images and feelings come to mind, holding them tenderly, and then letting them go into the "heart of compassion." "You can weep," he adds.)

The second morning of my meditation practice, I rolled out of bed and found my way to the same spot on the sofa. This time, the images that came were of Kelsey's life. I saw her birth and felt the prickling of my breast as I nursed her; I saw Craig and me dropping her off at college, and my heart constricted as we said goodbye; I saw Kelsey and me walking through the Washington Heights neighborhood of New York, and my breath caught as she told me about a sexual experience with a man who lived nearby. Again, I wept—and again, the session lasted for close to two hours.

After those two days, I meditated daily for about forty-five minutes to an hour. I never set a timer, just sat for as long as it felt right. My head was empty of coherent thought, the void filled by my breathing. Meditating became an essential part of my daily routine. Usually, I breathed my way to what I thought of as the *velvet place*, a welcoming darkness in which I felt enveloped, cared for, connected to something beyond myself, and—as though through a mist—also to Kelsey.

I incorporated other spiritual activities into my days, like taking walks on the beach and consciously trying to be present in the moment. I carried a camera with me to focus on the details of objects

---

[1] https://grateful.org

around me, taking fifty photos of one log, photographing the slow progress of a hermit crab as it moved from one shell to another, pointing my camera at a small bee in the center of a flower.

I don't know if it's because I'm concentrating so much on life, but I miss you a tiny bit less, Kelsey.

Well Mom, you're practicing a new way of seeing what is around you, and—although it may surprise you—that also means a new way of seeing me.

Because reading had been helpful to me in every crisis of my life and especially after Kelsey's death, I searched through Craig's extensive library for books that might give me spiritual insight. Tucked amid the tomes on philosophy, psychology, and theology, I discovered Alfred North Whitehead's *Process and Reality*. Craig had reworded a quote from Whitehead, the British mathematician and philosopher, during the dreadful hours after Kelsey's death: *Nothing is ultimately lost but gathered into God's infinite care and returned to us as possibility*. Those words had been a life saver amid the turbulence of initial grief.

I skimmed through *Process and Reality*, landing on certain phrases that spoke to me of God and of Kelsey. In Whitehead's words, God "persuades" opportunities to arise out of infinite potential, joining with us in an ongoing creative process. According to my interpretation of Whitehead's philosophy: God was not responsible for Kelsey's death but, to use a metaphor, was walking and weeping with me and continually offering new possibility. Both God and Kelsey, for it seemed they weren't separate, were present in Judith's suggestion that grieving might be a spiritual practice; both were present during my morning meditations; both were present in the leaf that waved to me each morning. And both proffered new ways for me to live my life.

I read *The Mystery of Death* by Ladislaus Boros, a mid-twentieth-century Jesuit theologian. Boros writes that body and soul cocreate each other throughout one's sojourn on Earth. The soul that sloughs off the body and lives beyond death is not at all the same as it was at birth. It has been transformed through its embodied experience. I loved the concept of body and soul cocreating each other, but I worried: *Did Kelsey's soul and body have enough time for cocreation during her relatively short life?* Theological questions were no longer intellectual exercises—they had emotional power and could either quiet my doubts or rouse new ones.

Whenever I was thrown off-balance by a theological query or comment, I remembered the reassurance of my dream the night after her memorial service in which Kelsey told me, albeit without words, that she was all right—in fact better than she had ever been. The apostle Paul wrote in 1 Corinthians 13:12, "For now we see through a glass, darkly; but then face to face: now I know in part; but then shall I know even as also I am known." Although I didn't have anything near a complete understanding—of course not—I knew she was fine. I didn't understand how to have the dynamic relationship I wanted with her, but I began to believe I'd find a way.

chapter nineteen
All Shall Be Well

Even though I was beginning to feel more hopeful, I continued to be retraumatized from time to time, such as when overhearing a chance remark about going on a bicycle trip, or seeing a mother and daughter together at a coffee shop, or watching an ambulance speeding to the scene of an accident. At those moments, I descended into the abyss.

"We want you to come to our cabin this summer," said Annie's mom, Holly, putting down her fork and looking at me intently. John, Annie's dad, leaned over the table, his long, lean frame bending like one of the Plasticene toys my kids used to play with. "Our cabin isn't far from Marrowstone. It'll take you only forty minutes to drive there."

"That'd be great," I said, trying to smile. I bit off a piece of sourdough roll and stared at my plate of roast chicken and kale salad, unsure whether I could eat any of it. Although Craig and I had met Holly and John before, this dinner at Sam and Annie's home was our first opportunity to get to know one another. The kids had been nervous about getting us together, uncertain whether we would get along. But Holly and John were easy to like—generous, kind, and fun—and they clearly adored our son. The rapport between Annie's parents and Sam made me glad, but also a tad jealous. Most of my recent conversations with Sam had been about misery and pain. I longed for our before-Kelsey's-death relationship but had no idea how to get back there or if doing so was even possible.

After dinner and coffee, we all said goodbye on the front porch, and the four of us parents walked down Sam and Annie's front steps. Just as he reached the bottom step, John abruptly turned around and called out, "Don't forget about our bicycle trip next weekend, Sam!"

"I've got it on the calendar," Sam replied with a smile.

They're planning a bicycle trip! I thought. The mere mention of "bicycle" was enough to make me break into a sweat and start shaking. But even worse, they were planning to have fun. Tears welled in my eyes. I hadn't had fun with Sam since Kelsey died. I couldn't imagine that I ever would again.

In the middle of the night, I awoke with a start. Maybe I'd had a bad dream, maybe I hadn't quite fallen asleep, but I had a vivid image of Sam and John on a bike trip, laughing and joking. My mouth felt dry. Trembling and sick to my stomach, I got out of bed, walked to the living room of our Seattle apartment, and stretched out on the couch. I tried to distract myself by concentrating on the lights across Lake Washington, visible through the windows, but that made me feel even worse. Every point of light seemed to come from a place where people were having fun. I felt completely alone. *I can't hold on to my children*, I thought. *They're disappearing one by one.*

But then, a sense of peace began to flow into my chest—a feeling of well-being that seemed to come from the deepest part within me and also from outside of me. The medieval anchorite Lady Julian of Norwich described it when she wrote in her journal: "All shall be well, and all shall be well, and all manner of thing shall be well." My belief in God had become blurry, drifting in and out of focus, but at that moment I felt what is best described by the apostle Paul in his letter to the Philippians (Philippians 4:7): "the peace of God, which passed all understanding."

The neural connections in my body were working overtime. An event such as overhearing Sam and John planning a bicycle trip transformed me, within milliseconds, from being relatively calm to despairing. Sensory perceptions could spark a plethora of memories. A ripple across the water reminded me of the dolphin-like movements of Kelsey in my womb. The softness of moss brought the memory of clasping her small hand as we walked through a park. The spicy scent of eucalyptus transported me to Monterey Bay and the family reunions that Kelsey so loved. Mint, parsley, and rosemary at the farmers market reminded me of a moment during the summer after Kelsey graduated from high school.

I was on my knees, weeding our herb garden, when Kelsey ran out of the house, grinning broadly, her eyes sparkling. "Mom! Guess what?" She paused dramatically. "I've been accepted into Columbia's Urban Experience program!" I inhaled sharply, realizing that meant she would leave for college a week sooner than I'd anticipated.

"That's great!" I said, wiping the dirt off my hands and hugging her. But my knees felt weak. *Oh my God*, I thought. *She really is going to leave home.* I had an unexpected sensation of loss, minor compared with death, but intense, nonetheless.

Once Kelsey's Urban Experience program was finished, Craig and I flew to New York to help her move into her dorm, bringing with us four enormous suitcases filled with the clothes, photos, and books she thought she would need for the year. We returned to Seattle a few days later with only two small carry-on bags. On our flight home, a sensation of emptiness crept into my chest. Why hadn't I anticipated how much it would hurt to leave Kelsey—and to have her leave us?

It didn't take long for me to adjust to Kelsey's absence. Sam and Max were still living at home and required my attention, and Kelsey's bubbly excitement about being in college and living in New York City was contagious. Craig and I phoned, emailed, and texted her every few days and visited her as often as possible, often finding work-related reasons to be in New York.

Three years later, when Sam enrolled at Columbia University's School of General Studies, we visited even more often, frequently going out for Ethiopian, Cuban, or Chinese meals—on rooftops, off alleys, and in the shadow of the Brooklyn Bridge. At times, our easy-flowing discussion devolved into an argument.

"Sam, you're frowning. Why don't you just say you're mad at me?" Kelsey asked during a dinner at a restaurant near Central Park.

"Stop, Kelsey! I'm not like you. I don't feel good about you right now, but I don't know what more to say. You keep pushing me to say more than I can."

Sam refused to eat in the Harlem restaurants Kelsey loved because he opposed the gentrification of the neighborhood. I railed against the misogyny of rap, and Sam said I misunderstood the genre. Our conversations were surprisingly heated and often ended up with Kelsey or me in tears—and all of us bewildered about how a peaceful family dinner could suddenly become as arduous as navigating through rapids. We were trying to work out new and complex adult-adult relationships, trying to figure out how we could let go of our old roles and still be close.

After Kelsey died, the dynamics became even more complicated. *How do we find our way through* this? *How can we still be a family with one of us in the world beyond?* I wondered. The questions triggered doubt—but also possibility. I didn't have a road map, but I believed we *could* grow and change as a family with Kelsey firmly in the mix.

chapter twenty
Travel and Pilgrimage

"I think we should take a trip to France," Craig said to me toward the end of the long, excruciating summer after Kelsey's death. "We always wanted to take a trip in the fall, but we never could while you worked. Now that you're taking a leave of absence, let's do it."

I emerged long enough from my ever-present state of fogginess to reply, "I can't even begin to think of traveling, unless we go to a monastery."

Craig raised his eyebrows and shrugged but—taking me at my word—began to research monasteries in France. A few days later, he reported back on what he'd discovered. There were monasteries that could accommodate us, but most of them housed men and women separately. "I have to tell you, sleeping on a narrow bed in a room with other men isn't what I had in mind," he said.

I agreed. We needed to be together, so a monastery was out of the question. But the idea of a trip—like onions caramelizing—was slowly becoming sweeter. I decided to regard this trip as a kind of pilgrimage, an extension of my spiritual practice.

As a young child, growing up amid the unending cornfields of central Illinois—rich black soil and the ubiquitous odor of manure—I dreamed of traveling. My dad regularly read *Gourmet* magazine cover to cover, writing down recipes and devouring articles about travel. During World War II, he was stationed first in Japan and then in China, thrilled to learn something about cultures so different from his own. But after the war and back in Illinois—with a small business and a growing family to feed—he couldn't afford the time or money for travel, yet he never lost his yearning to see the world. He liked to read the *Gourmet* essays on travel and food to Mom, and I paused whatever I was doing long enough to listen. I daydreamed about strolling through the streets of Paris, rummaging through book stalls along the Seine, and grabbing a baguette from the corner boulangerie, but the possibility of me visiting Paris or any of the other cities featured in *Gourmet* seemed remote.

One or two times a month, on Sundays following church, we drove forty miles to my grandparents' farm town—population four hundred—along a dreary two-lane highway with views of grain elevators and lonely barns—and without a single curve along the way. A slight buckling of asphalt midway through the trip had caught Dad's attention, and he remembered exactly where it was. "Here it comes, kids," he would say each time we got close, glancing at us through the rearview mirror. "Are you ready? Because we're coming to the mountains. On the other side is Santa Barbara and the Pacific Ocean." He inhaled deeply as if savoring the scent of the sea, and then asked, "Can you smell it? Can you smell the Pacific Ocean?" I closed my eyes. I thought I could detect, above the sharp odor of manure, the scent of salt water and seaweed. Following Kelsey's death, I remembered the exhilaration I'd experienced in the midst of Illinois cornfields, the visceral yearning to see the Pacific Ocean. *Would I ever regain my hunger for traveling*, I wondered?

I saw an ocean for the first time when I was seventeen. In the summer after my junior year of high school, I went to Türkiye as an exchange student. Each year my high school raised sufficient funds to send one or possibly two students abroad through the American Field Service exchange program. I had longed to be an exchange student ever since first hearing about the program when I was a freshman. Along with seven hundred other teenagers who'd been placed with families in Europe or the Middle East, I spent ten days crossing the Atlantic Ocean aboard the *MS Seven Seas*, formerly a World War II troop carrier for the US Navy. Shortly before I left, Dad drew me aside and said he'd written to Suleyman Atakoğlu, the father of my Turkish exchange family, and asked him to teach me about Islam. "And you can tell him about Jesus," Dad said. I nodded, but in truth I couldn't see that happening. Jesus was someone I'd learned about in Sunday school, someone my dad often spoke of, but to me he was more like one of my kidneys—something I took for granted, knew was important, but didn't really want to talk about.

The Atlantic Ocean was every bit as magnificent as I'd imagined. Salt spray on my face, sunlight sparkling on azure and white waves, starlight shining on ebony water. And being aboard with all those teenagers was totally fun. I experimented with a new persona: Whereas at home I was frenetically busy with school clubs and activities, while aboard ship I had absolutely no interest in joining a committee of any kind, choosing instead to swim leisurely laps in the pool and chat with friends over afternoon pastries.

We docked in Rotterdam, and those of us going to Türkiye took an overnight flight to Istanbul. I stayed up all night as we flew over mountain ranges and rivers whose names—the Alps, the Rhine, the Danube—were like magic. I had to pinch myself. There I was, a teenager from central Illinois who'd never been out of the Midwest, flying over places I'd only read about or seen in movies. It never crossed my mind to sleep.

My Turkish family was waiting for me at the airport gate: Suleyman, with an ample but compact belly, a thin grey mustache, and twinkling eyes; his smiling wife, Leman, dark-haired and plump; and Nazire, nineteen, with high cheek bones, dusky blonde hair, and blue-green eyes. The four of us, along with my shockingly enormous suitcase, crammed into a small yellow taxi that drove along a highway that skirted the Sea of Marmara. We slipped under a stone arch to enter the city and slowed to navigate narrow streets, crowded because of market day, the air scented by roasting lamb, ripe fruit, and an ancient sewage system.

The next morning— following the muezzin's call to prayer from the minaret of a nearby mosque —I walked into the dining room wearing a tiny gold cross on a chain, a parting gift from my grandma. A breakfast of briny white cheese, black olives, and a pretzel-shaped bagel called *simit* was spread on a lacy white cloth. A day later, after tasting an assortment of new foods and fighting off homesickness, I was felled by wave upon wave of diarrhea and spent hours staggering miserably from the toilet to bed. My Turkish mother finally decided it was time to intervene and walked into my bedroom carrying a plate with a single baked potato. Warm, earthy, and above all familiar, that potato was a miracle. My stomach settled, and the fog of homesickness lifted. Suddenly, I could see through the windows of the family flat what had been out of focus before: palaces that looked like lavishly decorated cakes, tall minarets with cone-shaped tops, the turquoise Bosphorus flowing into the blue-and-black Sea of Marmara.

When my family rented a house in a seaside village, a day's travel by ferry, train, and taxi from Istanbul, the owners of the house moved to the roof, and we occupied the rooms below. Nazire and I developed a routine of swimming and sunbathing in the mornings and strolling around town in the hot afternoons, eschewing the nap that was routine for the rest of the family. Sometimes, we caught a water taxi to a remote beach where we spent the entire day swimming and drinking tea in a beachside café.

I developed a crush on a Turkish medical student named Nazmi. He wasn't like any of the boys back home, and spending time with him was unlike any date I'd ever been on. To begin with, we were never alone—that wouldn't have been allowed in my Turkish family—so, instead, we walked amid gnarled olive trees and drank sweet tea in a café high above the sea, always accompanied by Nazire and sometimes by an additional friend or two. Nazmi was a Marxist and refused to drink Coca-Cola, telling me that it represented the ubiquitous evil of capitalism. (A decade later, when he was a practicing surgeon and still a Marxist, he fled Türkiye to escape imprisonment by the military junta and established residency in Germany.) Because of our conversations, I began to see the world in new and surprising ways—and to see my country in new and sometimes disturbing ways.

Following up on my dad's request, Suleyman invited me to sit with him one afternoon near the end of my visit, so he could teach me about Islam. He handed me a photo from his recent pilgrimage to Mecca in Saudi Arabia: He's standing in front of the House of Allah in a long white robe, and his face is radiant. *Suleyman is a good man,* I thought, *who loves Allah the way Dad loves Jesus.* That night I removed the necklace I always wore—the gold chain with a small, gold cross—and tucked it into a pocket of my suitcase. I never wore it again, and I never again believed that following Jesus is the only way to God.

Nazire and I lost touch within a few years. We both married, divorced, and married again; my parents moved; her parents died, and their house was sold. Although I tried to track her down, I always ran into dead ends. A year or so after Kelsey died, when I had an especially strong urge to find her, my brother Jim suggested I join Facebook. "It's probably the best chance you have of locating her," he said.

He was right. I did as he suggested and came across Nazire's profile within a few days. After weeks of back-and-forth messaging, we made plans to get together. Craig and I flew to France, took a train to Prague, and then a flight to Istanbul. One day, Nazire and I spent an afternoon together, just the two of us, meandering through Sultanahmet, the oldest district of Istanbul and where I had lived with Nazire's family fifty years earlier. We made our way to a café next to the rococo-style fountain that had been erected in 1728 to honor Sultan Ahmed III and ordered two glasses of strong, black tea. "I wish I had met your Kelsey," Nazire said wistfully.

"I wish so, too. I wasn't sure how you'd respond when you learned that Kelsey had died. Talking about death makes some people uncomfortable."

"We wouldn't be very good friends, let alone sisters, if we couldn't talk with each other about our sorrows," she replied. I hugged her. Of course Nazire would feel that way! There was a reason I had so wanted to find her again. I also talked with Kelsey about our reunion.

Now that I've found Nazire, you are the one missing. I wish with all my heart that the three of us—you, Nazire, and I—could be together in this magnificent city, chatting and drinking tea.

I can't drink tea with you of course, but I'm here, Mom.

The passion for travel that had blazed in my heart before Kelsey died, was almost eradicated by her death—but the memory of trips I'd taken with her burned brightly. In the summer before her freshman year in high school, the two of us traveled to Oaxaca, Mexico to study Spanish and explore the beautiful capitol city as well as the nearby villages that were dedicated to crafts such as rug weaving, wood carving, and pottery.

One day after class, Kelsey and I took a bus twenty miles south of Oaxaca to the town of Ocotlán de Morelos and toured the pottery studio of a well-known ceramicist. "What do you think of these clay sculptures? I asked Kelsey.

"I love them!"

We spent an hour or so deciding which ones to buy. Kelsey immediately picked the figure of a woman with a basket containing various fruits on her head, holding three enormous calla lilies in her right arm, and a large pineapple in her left—and wearing an expression of serene confidence. I selected an opera singer in a long flowing dress with a flower in her hair.

We made our way to the Temple of Santo Domingo de Guzmán, a former convent founded in the sixteenth century. Sunlight streamed through the windows, brightening the simply decorated, baroque interior. Several Indigenous women with long, black braids and smocks over their huipils, were perched on high scaffolding, meticulously restoring the ornamentation above the altar. According to a brochure available at the entrance, they were being taught the art of restoration by the well-known local painter, Rodolfo Morales. I got goosebumps as I watched the women who were working on the altar—while standing next to my teenage daughter. The women were growing more skilled with each stroke, and Kelsey was becoming more confident with each passing day.

We made our way back to the bus station while savoring the shockingly colorful red, blue, and yellow flowers, the pungent scent of wood fire mixed with sage, and the melodic sounds of Spanish floating above the more guttural Zapotec. Tired and sweaty but utterly contented, we waited for the bus that would take us back to Oaxaca.

Every seat was occupied, and folks were standing in the aisle. A short, sturdy woman with a bright scarf tied around her hair slowly mounted the steps—a chicken tucked under one arm and a basket of mangoes balanced on the other. Just as she reached the last step, a few of the mangoes escaped and wobbled down the center aisle, one of them coming to rest at the foot of the man who was seated across from Kelsey and me. With a broad grin, he bent down to retrieve it. The chicken, gripped more tightly by its owner, squawked in protest, and the passengers burst into laughter. My heart swelled. I wanted that moment—seated in a dusty, crowded Oaxacan bus with my daughter by my side—to last forever.

A year or so after her death, I asked Kelsey, *Do you remember the bus ride from Ocatlán to Oaxaca when the chicken squawked and everyone on the bus laughed?*

I do!

That moment seemed like a touch of the Eternal. Now that you are part of the Eternal, does that make any sense?

Hey Mom, we're all *part of the Eternal. And like on that bus in Oaxaca, I'm next to you.*

At the end of that long, hard summer after Kelsey's death, Craig and I flew to Paris. Since we couldn't cope with reminders of previous family trips to Paris, we rented a house outside the city, in a village on a bend of the Seine. Absolutely by chance—although I now wonder if there *is* such a thing as coincidence—the house was only a mile from where Craig's best friend from childhood and his wife lived.

On our first day there, we went to lunch with Craig's friend, his wife, and her Romanian aunt and uncle. Seated next to the aunt, who didn't speak English, I had to rely on my rusty French. The longer we spoke, the easier our conversation became. I was surprised to discover that my head felt lighter, and I could breathe more easily. I even laughed from time to time. By concentrating on French nouns rather than on death, on French verbs rather than on grieving, I felt better. Throughout the rest of the trip, I took advantage of every opportunity to speak French.

One morning, we took an excursion by car outside Île de France, the region surrounding Paris, and drove for miles with nothing on the horizon but low clouds, until we rounded a bend and there, soaring high above the fields of wheat, was the magnificent Cathédrale Notre-Dame de Chartres. My heart leapt. Craig and I had visited the cathedral on our honeymoon, and we took our kids to see it fourteen years later. On this trip, three months after Kelsey's death, I wanted to see the recent restoration of the cathedral, but I also wondered what I might discover spiritually in that magnificent structure. *A new understanding of God? A way to Kelsey?*

The cathedral walls were a soft ochre. The medieval sculptures—apostles, saints, and the Holy Family—had been so meticulously cleaned that I could discern subtleties in their facial expressions: a sardonic grin, a wrathful glare, a gaze of sorrowfulness. I stood, transfixed, in front of the stone carving of Mary with her arms curled around her baby and an expression of boundless love on her face.

After trying to catch a glimpse of the famous Chartres labyrinth, hidden under rows of chairs but open for meditative walking on Fridays from Lent until All Saints Day, I seated myself in a pew toward the nave's center and gazed up at the rose window, marveling at the intense cobalt blue. I felt an inner peace, a warmth that filled me with a sense of being closely held despite the soaring ceiling. And I had one of my many conversations with Kelsey:

Sitting here in this beautiful cathedral, I have a sense of Divine presence—and of you. It may just be wishful thinking, but...

I'm here.

When the cathedral caught fire in the late twelfth century, monks emerged from the glowing embers bearing the unscathed relic: a fragment of the tunic Mary was wearing when she gave birth to Jesus. As word of this miracle spread throughout Europe, sufficient money was raised to hire all the carpenters, stonemasons, sculptors, glaziers, and glass painters necessary for rebuilding the cathedral. This meant its reconstruction could be completed in just twenty-six years—compared with the almost two hundred years it took to build Notre Dame in Paris. I was interested in discovering how the town of Chartres originally obtained a piece of Mary's garment—an intrigue all its own—but the relic, itself, meant nothing to me. I was in awe, however, of the many people who believed in miracles. I wanted a miracle in my own life.

One afternoon, a week or so following our visit to Chartres, I was by sitting by myself in a small hotel in the fishing town of Douarnenez—on the Crozon peninsula of western Brittany. Earlier in the day, Craig and I had walked around the old port and discovered, on almost every corner, a plaque or a statue for someone lost at sea or killed in a cannery accident. (Douarnenez has been home to sardine fishermen and cannery workers for centuries.) As I gazed out the window at the turquoise and blue water of the bay, I found myself thinking about the town mothers who'd lost their children to the sea. All at once, I felt their arms around me like Mary's arms around her baby. A rush of relief coursed through my body: I was with other bereaved mothers who fully understood my pain. The sensation lasted only seconds, far less than a minute. I sat still for a while afterward, shaking my head in wonder, but mostly trying to capture the sensation of arms around me, the rush of compassion that I'd felt in the presence of the mothers of Douarnenez. I glanced once more toward the bay and hurried back to our room.

"You won't believe what just happened to me!" I said, flinging open the door. Craig looked up from the book he was reading and studied my face.

"You had a vision of some sort."

"How did you know?"

"By the look on your face."

After I described my experience, he smiled. "It makes sense," he said, "This place has seen so much loss. Of course, you would feel the presence of the mothers."

As we drove out of Douarnenez the next day, I remembered how it had felt to be in the *spiritual* presence of grieving mothers. Unexpectedly, I felt an intense empathy for the many *flesh-and-blood* mothers who had lost their children. Until that moment, I hadn't been able to bear their pain along with my own, nor had I been ready to fully accept I was one of them—but suddenly I found myself yearning to be with them, longing to not only receive but also *give* support.

Craig and I continued on to Carnac in northeastern Brittany to view the megaliths, ancient stone structures, many of them still standing, constructed by the dwellers of the region seven thousand years before. While standing within a ring of *menhirs*—stones that had been placed in a circular arrangement, possibly for venerating the sun or some other kind of divinity—I sank to my knees, sensing an energy that was so palpable I could almost taste it. The words to "Elohai N'Shamah" the Jewish prayer sung by Debbie Friedman that had sustained me in the days following Kelsey's death, resonated in my head: "The soul You have given me is a pure one, and within me You sustain it."

For several years after Kelsey's death, a friend and I regularly walked a labyrinth on Marrowstone that had been modeled on the labyrinth at Chartres cathedral—a convoluted, stone-tiled path that traverses eleven concentric circles on its way to the center. The Marrowstone labyrinth, in a meadow adjacent to Fort Flagler State Park, is constructed of fir rounds, a foot apart, with lavender and calendula between them.

Before beginning our walk, my friend and I set our individual intentions—mine almost always to be open to the Spirit and to

Kelsey—then we embarked, one in front of the other, on the curving path. At one point, the trail came so close to the center. I thought I had arrived, but then it veered and took me in the opposite direction. Lucy Clark Ellman, in her website, *A Sacred Journey*[2], lists the following components for a mini-pilgrimage: "make the time; find the place; set your intention; slow down; seek out inspiration; spend time in reflection; connect with God; listen to what's stirring; and trust the process."

Once I actually reached the center, I seated myself on the large flat stone, took deep breaths of the woodsy air, and felt myself merging into meadow, trees, birdsong, and sky. And I had a conversation with Kelsey, the essence of which was this:

Are you here?
I'm here.

---

chapter twenty-one
Judaism and "Kaddish"

During that first year after Kelsey died, it was the thought of coffee that got me out of bed. Only a hint of not-yet-dawn light crept through the open window as I settled on one end of the couch in our Marrowstone living room, the coffee pot on the table next to me. I looked out the French doors and could just discern the shapes of the tall cedars and maples at the edge of the forest and the garden post on which an evergreen clematis weaved its circuitous path. Following a schedule inspired by the Benedictine monks, my intention was to spend my mornings in meditation and study and my afternoons working. As sunlight slowly filled the room, I finished meditating, turned off the lamp, and picked up a book. After reading a chapter or two, I wrote for a while in the small notebook I kept next to my books—I'd filled so many notebooks since Kelsey died, writing about whatever the reading stirred in me, trying to articulate my thoughts and questions.

I usually had finished my practice by the time Craig was taking his first sip of coffee. I shared my insights from earlier in the morning, and he contributed his perspective, honed by years of studying theology and, of course, informed by his own sorrow. We often talked for the rest of the morning and sometimes well past noon.

During the later afternoons, I worked, which is to say I did whatever was necessary to keep the corporeal aspects of our life together: laundry, shopping, cleaning, going to the bank. After Kelsey died, I took a leave of absence from my job advising special education teachers and school administrators in Seattle Public Schools. When the leave ended, I decided to retire nine months earlier than I'd planned, although I continued to lead occasional workshops on the impact of emotional trauma. (After Kelsey's death, I had a deeper, much more personal understanding of trauma.) Being mostly retired suited me. I appreciated having hours for meditating, reading, writing, and long conversations with Craig. Even though I'd enjoyed my work and missed my colleagues, my well-being was increasingly dependent on my spiritual practice.

Books on spirituality and grief were stacked on my nightstand. The pile grew so high they formed a tower rising from the floor, and then another and another until towers of books lined one wall. Some of the books were gifts, others I had purchased or borrowed because of a friend's recommendation or a reference in another book. Enthralled by a single line of Walt Whitman— "All goes onward and outward, nothing collapses"—I read his entire long poem, "Song of Myself." A few words from Anne Morrow Lindbergh about the fragility of a new relationship with a deceased child sent me in search of her diary, *Hour of Gold, Hour of Lead*. I read *The Complete Poems of Emily Dickinson* cover to cover—she was truly acquainted with death—and a few books on quantum physics. I loved the concept that light (and maybe Kelsey) could be simultaneously wave and particle.

I was in bed one night, reading a book I'd culled from Kelsey's collection of psychology texts, mildly interested in what I was reading but not totally engrossed. Then I came upon a sentence that made me feel like I'd been shocked by a fraying electrical cord. The author casually mentioned the "psychological immaturity" of those of his patients who believed in God. *You arrogant bastard!* I thought, but within seconds, I was spiraling downward, my whole body shaking. *Maybe I am psychologically immature; maybe I am afraid to accept reality; maybe there is no way for me to have a continuing connection with Kelsey.* I shoved the offending volume to the edge of my bedside table and reached for another book, one that had been recommended by a Buddhist friend. The lotus on the cover drew me in, and I opened to the first page. Suddenly, I felt a kind of inner *swoosh,* and heat flooded the center of my chest.

Kelsey!

Yes, Mom, it's me. Read this.

I read Jack Kornfield's book *The Wise Heart: A Guide to the Universal Teachings of Buddhist Psychology* well into the night. Although I searched the index looking for entries that might reassure me about the existence of God or the continuing existence of Kelsey, I couldn't find any. I did, however, find relief in Kornfield's gentle compassion and in his teachings about the spiritual aspects of the human journey through birth, death, joy, and sorrow.

When Judith suggested I attend her weekly Buddhist sangha on Capitol Hill in Seattle, I went, hopeful of finding further help with my own journey through sorrow. The large hall was empty except for a makeshift altar next to one wall. A few men and many more women were positioning cushions on the floor for a group meditation. I nodded to a few acquaintances and hugged a good friend whom I hadn't expected to see there. The leader of the group rang a bell, and the chattering ceased. Once all of us were seated, she began a short, guided meditation that led into a lengthier silent meditation. Afterward, someone volunteered to lead the metta prayer:

> *May I (you, all beings) be filled with loving kindness.*
> *May I (you, all beings) be safe from inner and outer dangers.*
> *May I (you, all beings) be well in body and mind.*
> *May I (you, all beings) be at ease and happy.*

The metta prayer, said regularly, develops one's capacity to extend loving kindness throughout the world, in the process transforming oneself and making the planet a better place. Prior to Kelsey's death, I happily would have tried to make metta a part of my own practice. After her death, the central belief—that the prayer brings kindness, ease, and *safety* to others—made me angry. *Why wasn't Kelsey kept safe?* I wondered. *Are others more deserving of protection?*

We then broke into small groups to share individual concerns. I listened to the other members of my small group tell what was troubling them: "I yelled at my kids who are driving me nuts." "The dog ripped up my favorite dress." "We can't decide where we should go for spring break." I felt like I was living on an entirely different planet from these people and their concerns. Nevertheless, I decided to share what weighed on my heart—*Buddhism is about the entire human journey, including death, is it not?* I swallowed hard and said in a trembling voice, "My daughter died in June, and I don't even know how to put one foot in front of the other."

After a pause during which no one said a word, a small middle-aged woman tilted her head and looked at me with raised eyebrows. "You should be in a grief group." Although she didn't say it, I could hear her next words in my head: *Not* here.

I froze. *That's it*, I thought, determined never again to set foot in that sangha. The friend I had unexpectedly met that morning said to me later, "Oh, that's just Mary." But I didn't have the capacity to extend loving kindness to Mary; I was too much in need of it myself. And I'd felt totally out of place among people with whom I no longer had anything in common. I gave up on the sangha but not on Buddhism and devoured books written by Western Buddhists such as Sharon Salzberg, Jon Kabat-Zinn, Pema Chödron, and, of course, Jack Kornfield.

My friend Pam suggested that we go together to a meditation workshop led by Jack Kornfield at Spirit Rock Meditation Center in the hills of West Marin County, California. Just as I treasured Jack Kornfield's writing, I adored his gentle guidance through the morning meditation. In the afternoon, each of us was invited to share a concern during a private, ten-minute session with one of several experienced Buddhist practitioners. I chose to meet with a Buddhist psychologist, trained in working with trauma, hoping that she could help me become less triggered by reminders of Kelsey's accident. We met in a small cottage not far from the main building. Two wooden chairs faced each other in the center of the room, and a wall of windows afforded a view of the surrounding trees. A small dark-haired woman opened the door, uttered a brief welcome, and invited me to sit down. I launched into my story:

"My daughter died in a bicycle accident last June, and I can't stop thinking about it. I'm hoping you can help me be less triggered by reminders of her accident."

She nodded in reply and then stated, "I think you should pray metta for all bicyclists by saying, 'May all bicyclists be safe.'"

I was dumbfounded. I'd expected a few words of sympathy, an acknowledgment of how difficult it must be to lose a child. Instead, she merely suggested a rote practice, one that already had given me difficulty. A ball of anger exploded in my chest. "Why should I do that?" I said coldly, not caring that I was probably breaking Buddhist rules of decorum and almost certainly offending this woman.

Her eyes widened. "You want everyone to be safe, don't you?"

"Why wasn't my daughter kept safe? Did she deserve to die? Are others more deserving of life? No, I certainly won't pray metta for all bicyclists. It doesn't work or at least it didn't for my daughter." *And you didn't see me or my pain,* I added silently.

She looked at me in horror as I stumbled out of the cottage. "She calls herself a trauma therapist!" I muttered to myself as I tried to slow my steps in sync with a walking meditation. My palms were sweaty, and my neck felt rigid. I was surprised by the strength of my rage and shocked that it had come out at Spirit Rock. As I walked along the worn path, under the clear sky and sheltering pines, I realized that I needed a different spiritual path. Buddhism, especially mindfulness meditation, had been and still was immensely helpful, but I wasn't ready yet to relinquish my sadness. It seemed inextricably linked to my love for Kelsey.

A few days later, a friend and I walked around Green Lake under a dark sky that threatened rain. I told her about my experiences with Buddhism. She turned to me, her eyes shining with excitement, and asked, "Do you want to join a class in Jewish mysticism at our synagogue?" My heart skipped a beat. She continued, "The teacher is fabulous. She was awarded a prestigious grant to study Jewish mysticism with scholars in both the United States and Israel, but she's very down-to-earth."

I knew about both Christian and Sufi mysticism, but I didn't think there was such a thing as Jewish mysticism. "Yes, I'd love to join your class," I said, feeling a new looseness in my chest, "but will it be okay since I'm not Jewish?"

"Of course. I'll let her know you're coming."

Dressed in jeans and a plaid shirt, Beth looked more like a teenager than a well-regarded scholar of Jewish mysticism. Her warm welcome loosened the knot in my stomach and reassured me that I wasn't intruding. The class met once a week in the book-lined study of the synagogue. About a dozen of us, mostly women, sat around two long tables, reading texts written by Jewish mystics such as the Baal Shem Tov, the eighteenth-century Polish rabbi who founded Hasidism. We read passages from the Talmud, rabbinic teachings that had been compiled in the second through fifth centuries, and writings from the Midrash, a way of interpreting the first five books of the Bible through insightful stories. For the few of us who didn't know Hebrew, Beth provided English translations.

In response to one of the texts, a woman spoke of her intense sadness over the death of her ninety-five-year-old father. No one said, "Well, he had a long life." No one tried to talk her out of her sorrow. *I'm with my people!* I thought. Even when we read stories from the Bible that I knew well, it seemed as though I was reading them for the first time, such as this story found in Leviticus 10:1-2:

> *Now Nadab and Abihu, the sons of Aaron, each took his censer and put fire in it and laid incense on it and offered unauthorized fire before the Lord, which he had not commanded them. And fire came out from the Lord and consumed them, and they died before the Lord. Then Moses said to Aaron, 'This is what the Lord has said: Among those who are near me I will be sanctified, and before all the people I will be glorified.' And Aaron held his peace.*

Even though, presumably, the Lord had killed his children, Aaron said nothing. According to Beth, scholars haven't known quite what to make of his silence, but as I remembered the mostly silent ride back to Seattle after Craig and I learned of Kelsey's death, it seemed clear that after the sudden death of his two sons, in silence was Aaron's only possible response. I felt a strong bond with him. *My man, Aaron!*

A woman from the class made a comment about "Jacob's dysfunctional family." I wondered what the heck she was talking about because, for me, Jacob and his family were just names in the book of Genesis, far removed from my life. My Sunday school teachers had tried to make characters from the Bible more real by using felt cutouts, but that hadn't worked. The same woman went on to talk about Jacob and his family—Isaac, Esau, Leah, Rachel—like she knew them, like they lived just down the street from her. It turned out, she'd read stories about them for years, not just from the Torah but also from the Midrash.

Scholarly rabbis in a time of theological creativity between approximately the third and twelfth centuries wrote interpretations of the Torah using a method called *midrash* that involved making meaning of individual letters and words and even the space between words. *Interpreting the space between words!* It felt to me like interpreting the liminal space between this world and the next—which was exactly what I wanted to do. Interpretations of biblical stories, during that fertile period, came to be known as the *Midrash Aggadah* or simply, *the Midrash.* They went far beyond the actual biblical words, elaborating on them, bringing them to life in new ways. The stories were extraordinary, but when read along with portions of the Midrash, they became more complex, astute, layered, and even strange in the way that all great stories are.

The medieval French rabbi known by the acronym, *Rashi,* wrote a commentary on Jacob's dream with angels both ascending and descending a ladder. Rashi speculated that the angels were rising from Earth to tell God what was going on and coming down from Heaven to convey God's response—an ongoing conversation between Jacob and God relayed by the angels! The commentary felt like an invitation for me to speak with Kelsey—my own angel.

I needed to go beyond the facts around Kelsey's accident because the facts themselves were getting me down. At the time of her death, the police took her bag into custody in case it could provide information for their investigation. In late spring, when almost a year had passed since Kelsey died, I contacted our attorney, my heart in my throat, to ask when to expect the report. Did I really want to know what caused her death? Would we sue if someone were found to be at fault? I didn't know the answers to those questions, but I knew that I didn't want Kelsey's bag to be left in a Boston police station. A few days later, our attorney put the bag in the mail. Apparently, the police no longer needed it.

Because Craig was out of town when the box with the bag in it arrived, I asked Sam to come to our apartment to help me open and sort through it. Just seeing the bag was devastating. The outside was stained by blood; the inside contained Kelsey's phone, her wallet, a receipt from the dinner she and Ada had shared before the accident, and a single gold earring. The immediate impact of seeing the bag catapulted me back to the moment of learning of Kelsey's death and to the first days of overwhelming grief. I was weary from the repetitiveness of my feelings, but apparently, they weren't finished with me. I stuffed the bag into the back of a drawer and tried to forget about it.

Although we never received a written report, the police finally called our attorney and relayed their findings to him: There were no witnesses. No one on the bus had been aware of hitting Kelsey, including the driver. There was no one to point a finger at. The accident had been just an accident.

Sometime in the first months after her death, I had a dream in which I asked Kelsey to tell me what happened. She told me—in the dream—that she fell and looked up to see the bus approaching. I've accepted that's what happened—although it's still a mystery how she fell and why the driver hadn't seen her. I once saw a bus run a red light. *Maybe that's what happened,* I thought. *Maybe Kelsey was crossing the street, and the bus ran a red light.* But, instead of discovering the facts surrounding Kelsey's accident, what I really wanted to do was to interpret my embryonic sense of our continuing relationship. I wanted to pay attention to the space between and beyond not only the *words* but also the *worlds*.

Max's baccalaureate was held on the first of June, the first anniversary of Kelsey's death. I watched him proceed down the aisle of the amphitheater in Swarthmore's lush arboretum and take his place among the graduating seniors, clapping as hard as I could to let him know how proud I was of him, how much I admired—and adored—him. Despite his intense sadness, he'd managed to keep up his grades and complete a huge project for one of his professors—editing entries from students in universities around the world as part of an international data base on nonviolent protest movements in almost every country of the world. No small task.

Sam specifically asked me *not* to talk about the anniversary of Kelsey's death, so as to make the day a celebration for Max rather than a marker of our loss. Although that approach made sense to me, texts poured into my phone from friends and family members as they observed the anniversary along with us. I tried to show a few of the texts to Sam, but he didn't want to look at them. Since I knew how it felt to have a sister die, I thought I understood his feelings. Kelsey was dead, but he and Max were alive—and Sam wanted to get on with living. I tried to remain silent about the anniversary, but it was ever-present in my thoughts.

That evening, as Craig, Max, Sam, Annie, Luke, and I walked to an Italian restaurant for dinner, I looked closely at the hundred-year-old houses and stopped to take in the fragrance of the early-summer flowering shrubbery, trying to force myself into the present moment, trying to forget the death that was always on my mind. I couldn't seem to get my feet solidly on the sidewalk. It felt like I was a fraction of an inch above the earth.

As darkness approached, we spread a blanket on the sloping lawn in front of the college administration building and watched the celebratory fireworks. They seemed fitting for the first anniversary of Kelsey's death—like memorial candles brilliantly lighting up the darkness. In Jewish tradition, the Mourner's Kaddish—a prayer in Aramaic stemming from the thirteenth century—is prayed for eleven months after the death of a loved one and on each subsequent anniversary, often accompanied by lighting a *Yahrzeit* candle. The Mourner's Kaddish speaks about faith in a time of emotional and spiritual darkness and affirms that even when it seems like God is nowhere to be found, the Divine is still central to our lives. I especially love this stanza of the American poet Marge Piercy's poem, "Kaddish":

> *Blessed is the word that cannot say the glory*
> *that shines through us and remains to shine*
> *flowing past distant suns on the way to forever.*

On the first anniversary of Kelsey's death, although I often felt separated from both God and Kelsey, although I couldn't feel my feet on the ground, hope for a better day was beginning to shine through the darkness.

chapter twenty-two
Back in Brooklyn

I grabbed the camera from my suitcase, stuffed the hotel key into my pocket, and strode purposefully through the brick-walled lobby. The hotel, once a warehouse, was in the gentrifying industrial district of Greenpoint, Brooklyn. The street outside the hotel was home to several factories that hadn't yet been turned into classy condos, but I could see it coming. I headed to a bakery recommended by the hotel receptionist for a to-go cup of coffee and a Polish pastry.

I'd come to the city to lead a workshop on the impact of emotional trauma, but I couldn't bear to stay anywhere that reminded me of Kelsey, choosing instead to stay in a hotel in Greenpoint, where I'd never been and where I knew no one. Kelsey's friend Naima had grown up in Greenpoint and written a novel about the impact of gentrification on her neighborhood. But she no longer lived there.

Greenpoint was teeming with bikes. They were everywhere: rolling along busy Manhattan and Greenpoint avenues, crowded on porches and in alleyways, and parked in front of stores where they displayed, just below the handlebars, small signs that advertised quick deliveries. I spent the next few hours creating a photo montage of bicycles, confronting head-on the objects into which I'd channeled much of my rage over Kelsey's accident.

Since I had a couple of days before my workshop, I resolved to use the time for writing. I walked a few blocks to a bookstore on Manhattan Avenue and bought a large yellow notebook and a package of ballpoint pens. I was afraid that I might forget Kelsey, might not remember facets of her life and our life together. I sat down on the loveseat in my hotel room. The room was spacious—at least by New York City standards—but warm and cozy. The walls were a light-red brick, and two or three lamps had been placed on tables around the room, giving off a soft glow. This protective nest seemed like the perfect place in which to record my memories. I opened the notebook and started writing. One image led to another. I could barely write fast enough. I felt Kelsey next to me, reminding me of things I may have forgotten.

Write about how much I loved working on the school newspaper.
Okay.
Don't forget about me being a camp counselor on Orcas Island.
Okay.
Remember how thrilled I was to move from the room I shared with Sam into my own room?
Of course! You were so excited, you practically somersaulted down the hall. I remember you placing each of your books on the shelf and then closing the door, so we'd all know that it was your *room.*

I wrote with dedication, taking breaks only to go to the bathroom or to stretch. I inhaled deeply as if in the middle of a forest rather than in a hotel room, exhilarated by my ongoing conversation with Kelsey. After nine hours, I was exhausted. I didn't really want to be around other people, so I got a bagel and an apple from a nearby store and brought them back to the room. That's when the tears began. All the emotions that had been triggered by the writing seemed to have been waiting for the right time. I sobbed, dried my tears, and sobbed again. It was hard to eat, hard to read, hard to do anything but cry. I went to bed early and, surprisingly, slept more soundly than I'd slept for days, even for weeks.

The next morning, while munching on the remains of the previous night's bagel and drinking a mug of hotel coffee, I looked at the last page I'd written and began all over again, eventually filling the thick notebook. Again, Kelsey was with me. Sometimes, I had questions for her:

Were you in love with Fernando? How about Jose?

I closed my eyes and was surprised to find the answers flowing into my head and then from my head into the notebook. *Is Kelsey really giving me this information?* I shrugged. I had no idea how I could be having a back-and-forth conversation with my dead daughter, but there it was.

I felt like I'd just finished swimming a mile: tired but satisfied. I closed the notebook and packed it at the bottom of my suitcase. Once home, it went into a drawer, and although I looked at it from time to time, I knew I'd never forget the memories inside. Even if I became senile—no longer remembering names, dates, what state I lived in, or who was president–my memories of Kelsey would remain integral to me, part of every cell in my body.

I realized that my memories weren't static—they had changed between the time of Kelsey's death and the moment of my writing them down, even just a few days later. Whenever *I* changed, my memories changed. I saw additional aspects to them, viewed them in new ways. They were like a dialogue between my brain and my heart, my past and my present, my body and my spirit, and—especially—between Kelsey and me.

The process of sitting in my Greenpoint hotel room, writing for two days, was a sacred ritual. Perhaps the biblical storytellers understood that their texts, like my memories, would be interpreted and reinterpreted over time. In my class on Jewish mysticism, I'd learned about PaRDeS, a method for interpreting the Torah in use since the Middle Ages. The word, *Pardes*, which means "orchard" in Hebrew, was a metaphor for Divine secrets, and PaRDeS is an acronym for four levels of interpretation: *peshat, remez, derash*, and *sod*. The first level is where one considers the literal meaning, often found in the root of the word. The second level involves looking for hints or possibilities that go beyond the straightforward; on the third level, one considers how the text may be allegorical or metaphorical; and on the last level of interpretation, one looks for what is hidden or secret.

I realized that I could use *PaRDeS* to interpret the intertwining of memories and grief. On the first level were the bare facts. The factual content—the who, what, when, and where—seemed to fade over time unless I wrote it down. I was beginning to understand, however, that the facts were only part of my memories, maybe not even the most important part. I also needed to go beyond the facts. What were the psychological aspects, for example, of a dinner during which Sam spent much of the time scowling and Kelsey was in tears? What did it mean when I went shopping with Kelsey and nothing that I liked appealed to her? And how had my sense of loss changed the facts? How had sadness altered my memories?

Skipping for a moment the third level and going to the last, I realized that in the days and weeks immediately after Kelsey's death, I was constantly looking for what was hidden or secret. I saw signs of Kelsey everywhere. When looking at rocks on the beach, one seemed to dance in front of my eyes. *Kelsey?* In an email draft on my computer, the word, *Kelsey*, was highlighted. I hadn't done it. The same leaf on the same tree waved to me each morning. *Kelsey?* The dreams of her that had come almost every night in the weeks following her death; the words on a page that seemed to hold special meaning; almost everything seemed to be a possible message from Kelsey. *Can I see what is secret if I look carefully enough? If I believe enough?*

What really startled me was looking at my memories from the level of the allegorical and metaphorical. A Buddhist allegory I'd read several times but paid little attention to, popped into my head, and stayed there because, apparently, I had something to learn from it. The main character of the story was a woman of privilege named Kisa Gotami whose only child died. To alleviate her suffering, she visited the Buddha and asked for help. He could help her, he said, but only if she returned to him with four or five mustard seeds from families who hadn't experienced death. Although she visited home after home, she couldn't obtain a single mustard seed: Everyone had been affected by death. Kisa Gotami at last understood that loss is an inextricable part of human existence. At the time of Kelsey's death, I, too, felt a sense of entitlement. The loss of a child wasn't supposed to happen to me. Because my parents had lost a child, I feared that I might as well, but another part of me believed, at least semiconsciously, that because I'd already experienced the death of a loved one, I wouldn't lose a child. Because I had a position of privilege as a White woman, I wouldn't experience the loss of a child as some of my Black friends and acquaintances had through death or incarceration. Before Kelsey died, I wasn't aware of this sense of entitlement, but when I eventually started asking, *Why not me?* I was amazed to find that my pain, like Kisa Gotami's, was lessened.

I was learning more about myself—and about my grief—through other stories as well. My mind returned again and again to a story we read in my class on Jewish mysticism. Kalonymus Kalman Shapira was a Hasidic rabbi in the Warsaw Ghetto during World War II who died in the last days of the uprising. Before he died, he wrote a letter to the members of his congregation, by this time starving and barely able to continue resisting the Nazi occupation. His letter survived the war. In it, he wrote that there are times so horrific that even God is overwhelmed and needs our help. "How in this present terrifying time can we help God when we can only just keep ourselves alive?" he asked his congregants. The answer was and remains this: Be kind to one another.

I realized that others, many others, have found the strength to endure—and have found meaning in the struggle by understanding that all of us share a burden of loss. And, when nothing else makes sense, when all seems lost, there is still the possibility of kindness, as American poet Naomi Shihab-Nye expresses beautifully in her poem, "Kindness":

> *Before you know kindness as the deepest thing inside,*
> *you must know sorrow as the other deepest thing.*
> *You must wake up with sorrow.*
> *You must speak to it till your voice*
> *catches the thread of all sorrows*
> *and you see the size of the cloth.*
> *Then it is only kindness that makes sense anymore.*

Soon after Kelsey died, I asked my mom what had sustained her when Sally died. She hesitated, her forehead furrowing, and then said, "The hardest part was finding out about her leukemia and watching her become sicker and sicker. But when she died? I don't know exactly. I leaned on your dad." A few weeks later, she came back to my question. "I've thought about it, and I remember your dad suggested I say the name of Jesus, so that's what I did, over and over. It helped. Just saying his name brought me peace."

I was sure that saying the name of Jesus wouldn't be of any use to me, but then I remembered a day when, deeply in pain, I walked along an island beach and began chanting words that I recognized as Hebrew but whose meaning I didn't know: "*Baruch atah Adonai Eloheinu melech ha'olam.*" The Hebrew words were comforting, and I said them over and over. Although I later learned their translation— "Blessed are you, Adonai our God"—and discovered that the words begin most Jewish blessings, the guttural yet also lilting sound of Hebrew and the vague knowledge that the words were holy rendered them powerful. And I understood at last how Mom had found peace by repeating the name of Jesus.

I had just finished several hours of taking photos up and down the streets of Greenpoint—a bicycle painted in psychedelic colors, a bicycle with a basketful of toys, an overabundance of bicycles on the stoop of an apartment building—when I stopped at a traffic light. A young man, wearing a bright green shirt and a baseball cap, was slowly pedaling *his* bicycle backward and forward trying to balance while waiting for the light to change. When he caught me looking at him, he broke into a grin. He and I were sharing a joke without words. I laughed, happy to be in this moment and place, even in the midst of my sorrow.

chapter twenty-three
Evening Star

"Stay away from trails at dusk, especially those with evidence of partially eaten salmon, bear scat, and clawed trees." The words on the can of bear spray made my shoulders tighten, but I stuffed the can into the pocket of my jacket and helped push the boat ashore. The sun was beginning to set as the two of us headed off on the trail, my friend Tom in the lead and me a few paces behind him. I glanced down and did a double take: carcasses of partially eaten salmon had been strewn up and down the path, and everywhere I looked, I saw bear scat. I turned to study the tree trunks on either side of me. Yep, there they were: claw marks. "Just how safe do you think this trail is?" I asked nervously.

Tom tugged down the brim of his *Headway Marine* baseball cap, left over from the boat-building company he once had owned and said casually, "Oh, I think we'll be okay."

Despite my uneasiness, we actually were *hoping* to spot bears, specifically spirit bears. Tom's wife and my friend Lise, who died of multiple myeloma six months after Kelsey's death, had longed to see a spirit bear. Our trip in the fall of 2013 was primarily to fulfill her dream—but I also wanted to deepen my spiritual practice. During the past few months, I'd been surprised to discover an inner bond with rocks, trees, eagles, and owls. So, a little more than year following Kelsey's death, Craig and I, along with Tom and another friend, Sallie, went to northern British Columbia in Tom's forty-two-foot wooden power cruiser *Evening Star* to search for spirit bears.

Spirit bears—a subspecies of black bear with a recessive gene that makes their fur white—live exclusively in the Great Bear Rainforest of upper British Columbia. For thousands of years these rare bears, thought to have spiritual power by the First Nations people, have encountered few humans other than members of the Gitga'at First Nation community and haven't yet learned to distrust humans. I've seen photographs of Gitga'at people lying next to and even cuddling the bears. There's a photo in the galley of *Evening Star* of one of the previous owners of the boat—a middle-aged woman—sitting next to a spirit bear, the two of them sharing lunch.

We searched for spirit bears using binoculars and sitting comfortably in the sun on the deck of *Evening Star* while anchored in a harbor of Princess Royal Island in the Great Bear Rainforest. Although I still felt the ache of loss, it was much less overwhelming in that beautiful harbor: Cottony clouds drifted across the sky. Still water mirrored towering trees. The cry of gulls on the rocky shore pierced the serene silence. A juvenile bald eagle sat on a branch of a nearby fir, motionless and staring straight ahead. A harbor seal bobbed up a few yards from the boat, then another appeared, and soon the entire pod was just off our stern. One of the seals surfaced with a large silver salmon flashing in its mouth. It nosed the salmon high in the air, and another seal caught and swallowed it. They continued this kind of volleyball, often lobbing the salmon so close to the boat we thought we might have to join in the game. Finally, they seemed to have their fill of fish and left us.

In the late afternoon, a pair of eagles joined the juvenile, still on the branch, and the three of them flew down to the beach, where they stayed, close together, for some time. We didn't really know their state of mind but wondered if the adults might be giving pointers to the young one, emboldening it to take a plunge or two in search of a meal. Or perhaps the entire time it spent on the branch, barely moving, was a kind of rite of passage. I thought about what it might take to parent a young eagle, giving it just enough guidance, not too much, not too little. I recalled the complicated dance that Craig and I engaged in as our own children were trying out their wings. We were able, for the most part, to allow them to learn from their failures as well as their successes. I felt proud of having raised our three children, pleased that we'd been able to help them navigate their transition into adulthood. As I watched the eagles, I thought about Kelsey—as I did so much of the time—reflecting on whether I could help her *now. How do you parent a dead child?* I wondered, although I was beginning to suspect it might boil down to love.

Coho salmon appeared to be running—the feasting seals were proof of that. We hoped that the abundant salmon would attract a hungry bear. The next morning, as the tide was coming in, we lowered a dinghy and two kayaks into the water. Craig and Tom got into the dinghy; Sallie and I climbed into the kayaks. Once we reached the shore at the mouth of a tidal creek, Tom decided to get out and wade through the water, protected by boots that reached almost to his knees. As we waited in the estuary for the tide to rise enough for us to paddle upstream, we were joined by such an abundance of salmon we couldn't see the creek bed. Once salmon enter an estuary with its mix of fresh and salt water, their color darkens from silver to red—and *these* ruby-colored salmon were close enough to touch as they swam in small circles next to our boats. I could sense their pent-up energy aching to be released, the narrowing of their focus as they waited for the tide to rise.

From time to time, an eagle swooped down and snatched a chunk of fish from the carcasses strewn across the rocks of the creek. I didn't know what had caused their death. A bear perhaps? This part of their journey didn't seem particularly dangerous, but maybe they had expended so much energy already that some of them could go no farther.

Sallie and I paddled—and Craig rowed—slowly up the creek in tandem with the salmon. Coppery sedge and emerald grasses bent in the breeze. The shrieking of gulls and the calls of ravens permeated the air. An unusual sound, a kind of purring, arose from the nearby forest. Sallie and I looked at each other nervously. "A cougar?" I asked.

Tom, a few yards away onshore, said, "No, not a cat—not sure what it is, but not a cat." Later, back onboard, we searched our field guides and discovered that among the raven's many calls it can emit a kind of low growl, almost a purr. No wonder the First Nations people have so many stories about the raven as a trickster.

We moved upstream with the salmon, maybe four or five yards at a time, and then waited for the tide. Such a long wait for such a short gain! At about noon, we reached the end of navigable water, blocked by jagged rocks that ascended fifteen feet or so. Salmon carcasses were strewn across the rocks and floating in the rock pools. This clearly *was* a dangerous segment of their journey. The Coho readied themselves by swimming in circles, gathering strength—it seemed—by contact with one another. One or two at a time, they began their ascent, hurling themselves over the treacherous rocks, resting in pools, and then doing it again and again. My heart hammered against my ribs. I couldn't take my eyes off the salmon, as I brushed away tears. I glanced at Sallie, who was dabbing her own eyes. No one said a word. I realized that it *is* possible to find the next world by paying close attention to this one. There is little, perhaps *no* separation between this life and the next—as the nineteenth-century English poet Elizabeth Barrett Browning states in her book-length poem, *Aurora Leigh*: "Earth's crammed with heaven - And every common bush afire with God." The salmon, heroically determined to spawn, were absolutely "afire with God."

Although we never found a spirit bear, doing so no longer mattered. After leaving the Great Bear Rainforest, we cruised through spellbinding fjords—forested cliffs above deep-blue water, clear sky with wisps of trailing clouds—on our way to the remote Gitga'at village of Hartley Bay. We tied *Evening Star* at the dock and began to explore, traipsing along the wooden planks that serve as both sidewalks and roads, stepping aside whenever a small all-terrain vehicle needed to pass. Ravens were ubiquitous in Hartley Bay, on pilings and rooftops, on branches of Douglas firs, and flying just above our heads, their calls sending chills down my spine, and their wingbeats, like the thrumming of a drum, making my spirit soar.

Upon returning home, Craig and I went to the studio of a Skokomish Indian sculptor who creates bentwood boxes of cedar using the traditional forms and shapes of Northwest Coast Indian art. We commissioned a box with Raven carved on the front as a remembrance of the trip—and a reminder that Earth is indeed "crammed with heaven."

The first Christmas after Kelsey's death, Craig started a tradition of filling her Christmas stocking—I couldn't bear to pack it away—with small gifts for each of us: a wooden bird, a small Indian pot, a piece of weaving, a poem. While searching for items to put into Kelsey's stocking a few years ago, Craig looked through the last journal she'd written in—all her journals, dating from preschool through graduate school, which I still haven't read, live in a large box in my closet. He discovered a section of the journal, written shortly before she moved from New York City to Boston. The words surrounded and were woven into an ink sketch of a tree. He made a copy of the drawing for each of us and placed them in her stocking. Her message was this:

> *"I'm growing my tree a little bit. Not uprooting, necessarily, just extending my branches. That's comforting, to think of not leaving behind everything I have here. I'm going to live up in the branches for a while, feel some new perspective from up there."*

The metaphor gave me pause—but it was comforting, too, and a perfect Christmas gift for each of us.

chapter twenty-four

"Art Thou in the Darkness?"

"When my daughter died, a year and a half ago everything I believed about God was destroyed in an instant. But I had visions and dreams that seemed to come from another world. I don't know if they were part of the Divine or if it was just grief talking." I was attending a three-day Quaker retreat, and each of the five participants in our small group had been asked to speak for fifteen minutes without interruption about a spiritual concern.

"Well maybe grief had a lot to do with it," said one of the group members, "but I sense that your experiences had a Divine source. It might take time for you to accept that you know what you know."

Since Kelsey died, I'd had mystical experiences that would be considered odd, even slightly unhinged, in the Protestant churches I'd gone to for most of my life. But I thought Quakers might have insight into the question: What is real and what is not? There was a sense of mysticism in the life and writings of the early Quakers like George Fox. In mid-seventeenth-century England, Fox had visions that prompted him to proclaim loudly and broadly that God speaks directly to each of us. He wrote in his journal: "Keep within. And when they say, 'Look here or look there is Christ,' go not forth. For Christ is within you, and all who try to draw your mind away from the teaching inside you are opposed to Christ. For the measure's within, and the light of God is within, and the pearl is within you, though hidden."

His preaching began a movement that eventually became the Religious Society of Friends. William Robinson was among those who, in the seventeenth century, brought this new religion from England to the American colonies. For his efforts, he was convicted and hung in Boston as a heretic, but his words—such as these which have been amended to reflect a more inclusive God—have inspired succeeding generations of Quakers: "The streams of my Father's love run daily through me. The streams of my Mother's love run daily through me. From the Holy Fountain of Life to the seed throughout the whole creation."

My first encounter with Quakers was in 1968 when I was twenty and newly arrived in Paris. With the intention of signing up to attend a Quaker camp the following summer, I took the metro to the Paris office of the American Friends Service Committee (AFSC)—a Quaker organization that, at the time, provided counseling to soldiers in the Vietnam War and ran peace camps throughout Europe. Astonishingly, in addition to registering me for a camp, the staff offered me the use of a tiny apartment in the sixteenth arrondissement with an Eiffel Tower view. The owner of the apartment, also an AFSC staff member, was on an extended family visit to South America. My rent would be covered by just a few hours of work in the office each week.

I stayed in the seventh-floor walk-up with a shared toilet down the hall, for three months (giving myself cold sponge baths and occasionally visiting a friend who possessed that rare commodity: a shower). Although I admired and was immensely grateful to the AFSC staff, I wasn't interested in attending a Quaker worship service or researching Quakerism. I was more given to luxuriating in my tiny, first-ever apartment, drinking wine with friends, and marching in the streets to protest the war.

Seven years later, when I was living on Orcas Island, I met a Quaker woman named Kathi. In her twenties and one of the most cheerful persons I'd ever met, she lived with her husband in a small hilltop cabin with a spectacular view but no plumbing or electricity. I happened upon her at the gas station one day as she was filling ten-gallon containers with water. In the course of our conversation, she mentioned that she'd grown up Quaker. By that time, I had attended services at one or two island churches, participated in a local Bible study, and gotten to know the Theosophists who ran a retreat center on the island. So far, nothing had satisfied my spiritual yearning. Her mention of "Quaker" stirred memories of the generous AFSC staff and awakened a latent interest in Quakerism. "How long have you been a Quaker?" I asked. "What do Quakers believe?"

Kathi laughed. "The best way to answer that last question is for us to meet in Quaker worship." The following Sunday morning, she and I pulled two chairs next to the fireplace in my small house and sat in complete silence for about an hour. At the end of the hour, Kathi quoted from Matthew 18:19–20: "For where two or three are gathered together in my name, there am I in the midst of them." The passage gave me goosebumps. Someone or *something* had been with us. Kathi and I continued meeting every Sunday for the next few months. Whatever was present in the silence, it spoke to my heart and gave me the courage to end my second marriage.

Following my divorce in 1977, I moved to an apartment in Seattle. Because I had a such a warm feeling about Quakers, stemming from the Sunday worships sessions on Orcas with Kathi, I decided to attend—along with my cousin Tricia and her husband, Steve—a Quaker meeting for worship in Seattle's University District. I expected that the meeting would be like what I'd experienced with Kathi: silence out of which I could hear an inner voice. However, as one person after another rose to speak, there was little time for silence. I was disappointed. Quakers believe that most of the inward messages one receives during a meeting for worship are intended for personal guidance, not for the entire group. Years later, a Quaker elder, with far more wisdom than I, told me, "You speak only when you have no other choice, when the Spirit almost lifts you to your feet." I wasn't sure why the meeting Tricia, Steve, and I attended had so much talk and so little silence, but I had no desire to return. Instead, I began attending Sunday services at Pilgrim Congregational Church where Craig was a minister and did so for the next ten years.

Quakers weren't on my radar again until twenty-five years later, when I attended a workshop inspired by the teachings of a longtime American Quaker and teacher, Parker Palmer, and learned about a process of discernment that had been developed by Quakers more than three hundred years earlier, called the "clearness committee". When someone is trying to decide something important—whether to take a particular job, for example—she or he invites a small circle of friends to meet. The group members listen respectfully, without interruption, to the concerns of the person in discernment and then ask open-ended questions like "Can you tell me more?" or "What makes you say that?" No one says, "I think this is what you should do." I was astounded by the wisdom of the early Quakers and impressed that the process had been followed for centuries.

I attended several early morning Quaker meetings for worship about a year later when Craig and I visited Max at Swarthmore College and stayed at Pendle Hill, a Quaker retreat center in an adjacent suburb. I loved those Pendle Hill meetings. Shortly after Craig and I returned to Seattle, a friend and I started a silent meeting at our church an hour before the regular Sunday service. Soon, I began skipping the regular service and going to a nearby café for coffee and a phone conversation with Kelsey—who was, almost always, also drinking coffee at a café near her apartment:

"Hi, sweetie! I just finished silent meeting. While I was sitting there, the Cat Stevens version of the hymn 'Morning Has Broken' went through my head, probably because you played it so often on our piano."

"How could I forget? I must have played ten times a day for a month while practicing for church."

"I thought of the song because of you, of course, but also because of the phrases, 'Mine is the sunlight, mine is the morning.' When I sing those words, I feel like I'm breathing in sunlight and am at one with the morning, especially the hours right around dawn."

"I've never been a fan of early mornings, but I do understand what you're saying."

About a year after her death, I received an email advertising Way of the Spirit, a program that offered a series of retreats focused on study, prayer, and contemplation "in the Quaker tradition." When I read "in the Quaker tradition," my heart raced. I definitely wanted to attend those retreats! I phoned the program's director and chatted with her for a while about my interest in Quakerism and then said, "I must tell you that my daughter was killed in a bicycle accident just over a year ago, and I'm still a mess. Do you think it would be okay for me to attend the retreats?"

"Yes, I think you'd be a wonderful fit—and we can accompany you in your grief," she responded. My heart soared with gratitude.

Sorrow never completely left me at any time during the Way of the Spirit retreats, but it wasn't central. I treasured the small group discussions when three or four of us met to respond to open-ended, spirit-related questions. And I loved learning how to *elder* another. The old Quakers thought of *eldering* as a way of monitoring and, when necessary, admonishing so as to keep fellow Quakers within established mores and traditions. A more modern concept of *eldering* is to provide a kind of spiritual companioning, suspending judgment and holding the person in Divine love and light. When I eldered someone as part of the Way of the Spirit retreats, I closed my eyes and opened to the Divine within me—a *place* that felt warm, accepting, and filled with energy—and allowed that energy to flow outward. Doing so required practice, but when I finally was able to put all the moving parts together, a transformation occurred in me and in the person being eldered.

Craig and I began attending a Quaker meeting in Port Townsend, a twenty-minute drive from our Marrowstone home. On our drive there, we crossed over the channel that divided Marrowstone and Indian Islands on a new bridge. The initial part of the bridge's construction involved removing truckload after truckload of the silt that had blocked the channel between Kilisut Harbor and Oak Bay for seventy-five years. As soon as the silt was gone, the channel was reestablished, and salmon once again began to pass through. The channel was named *Passage Through,* the English translation of a Klallam word.

Snow-covered mountains, the Cascades to the east and the Olympics to the west, rose above layers of blue-green hills. We drove past a small stand of Garry oaks, traversed another bridge, this one linking Indian Island with the mainland, passed by the Port Hadlock grocery store, veterinary clinic, and library; meandered along fields and forests and the Jefferson County International Airport, so named because of planes arriving from nearby British Columbia in Canada; slipped under an archway of Madrona branches; and entered Port Townsend. As we rounded a bend, we could see the Cascade Mountains soaring above the bay, sparkling in the sunlight, with scores of small boats and a large cruise ship on its way to Alaska. "I always love this view," Craig said.

In another five minutes, we were at the Quaker meetinghouse, a square white building with a gabled roof and a WAR IS NOT THE ANSWER sign near the front steps. We found our usual seats on a pew beneath the windows and joined in the silence. Wind rustled through the leaves outside, a Steller's jay trilled, a car motor hummed. Craig had one of his weekly conversations with Kelsey, which always began with, *Hey Kels, I'm here.* My occasional conversations with her during Sunday morning meetings for worship came like a hoped for but not counted on gift.

I worked on a committee responsible for the spiritual needs of the Port Townsend Friends Meeting and assumed an overall leadership role. Craig chaired a couple of committees but was happy to have *laid down* his former role of pastor and chaplain. There are so many ways that old Quaker expression can be used. Craig *laid down* his work as a pastor in a church and then as a chaplain to people who were mentally ill and without homes. I *laid down* being an educational consultant and workshop facilitator. Although I couldn't lay down my grief, I discovered a chant set to plainsong by Paulette Meier (using the words of seventeenth-century Quaker James Nayler) that reminded me to hold my pain lightly: "Art thou in the Darkness? Mind it not, for if thou dost, it will feed thee more. But stand still, and act not, and wait in patience, till light arises out of darkness and leads thee."

I was discerning how to "mind not" the darkness and beginning to trust that eventually the light would come—learning to balance sorrow with gladness, as beautifully illuminated by Mary Oliver's poem "Heavy":

> *Then said my friend Daniel,*
> *(brave even among lions),*
> *"It's not the weight you carry*
> *but how you carry it—*
> *books, bricks, grief—*
> *it's all in the way*
> *you embrace it, balance it, carry it*
> *when you cannot, and would not,*
> *put it down."*

I'd read the poem many times without really understanding the central point. Finally, I got it: Although some aspects of my grief would endure forever, I could learn the art of balancing.

chapter twenty-five
The Bicycle Trip

"There are so many wonderful ways of carrying children on bicycles," someone said at a family dinner party and then went on to detail all those "wonderful ways." I wanted to scream, *For God's sake, do not talk about bicycles!* Instead, I left the table and continued my imagined invective: *Bicycles trigger flashbacks of the accident that killed our daughter, and to make matters worse, our twenty-five-year-old son is on a solo cross-country bike trip. Please don't talk to me about bicycles and children.*

My brain was on Red Flag Warning, fearing a conflagration. It was the thirty-first day of Max's trip, with forty-six more to go. He'd left on Kelsey's birthday, March 17, and planned to return on the fourth anniversary of her death. The trip south along the West Coast from Seattle to San Diego and then east across the country was a long-dreamed-of adventure for Max—and a source of unending anxiety for me.

According to the Adventure Cycling Association, more than one thousand people bike across the United States each year, riding on wind-swept desert roads, over mountains, through cities and small towns, meeting new people and transforming their own minds and bodies. At least a few of them, like Max, are hoping to assuage their anguish along the way. Although I understood why Max was taking the trip, it didn't ease the vise tightening on my heart whenever I thought about it.

"What are you taking with you?" I asked Max when he came to our Marrowstone home for a test ride. He pointed to the pile of gear he was about to stuff into two shiny yellow paniers.

"You'll especially appreciate this, Mom," he said, holding up a lightweight green vest. "It's a reflecting vest, like you wanted, but unlike other vests this one won't make me too hot. I'll wear my orange rain jacket if it's raining. I'll be totally visible." I swallowed hard, trying to believe that the green vest would keep him safe.

Craig and I offered to accompany him in our Subaru as far as San Francisco. We told him we'd treat him to dinner each night, and he could sleep on the floor of our motel room. He agreed when he realized that sleeping on a dry floor during rainy March would be helpful as he built up his endurance. He also thought we might worry less if we saw what a capable and defensive rider he was.

In his bright vest and tight-fitting pants, and with the yellow paniers filled, Max looked nervous but excited. His cousin Benj—helmet in hand, hair damp from the ride to the ferry landing—had a huge grin on his face. He was planning to accompany Max on the first day—but then he needed to get back to work. The three of us were catching the 7:45 a.m. ferry to Bremerton. From there, the guys would head south, and I would drive north to pick up Craig. We planned to rendezvous later at our friends' home.

There was a seventeen-year age difference between Max and Benj, but they had developed a special relationship when Benj lived with us for a few years after college. Since Benj was an artist, he taught six-year-old Max how to draw and create installations. They drew murals on paper, wood, and long strips of melamine, and one summer they built a huge track for racing matchbox cars that ran the length of our large front yard. Benj hadn't been able to parlay his artistic abilities into a job, so he supported himself by repairing bikes, consequently kindling in his young cousin a love for all things bike related. I'm almost certain it was Benj who started Max dreaming about a cross-country trip, or at least he had a lot to do with the idea.

The Adventure Cycling Association has developed more than forty-five thousand miles of relatively safe routes within and between states as well as two that cross the country. The northern tier starts in Anacortes, Washington, passes through Idaho and Montana, scales the Continental Divide, continues through the prairie and midwestern states, and finishes on the coast of Maine—4,292 miles from the start. The southern tier, which Max was taking, begins in San Diego, heads east through the Arizona desert, climbs over the Continental Divide in New Mexico, crosses arid West Texas and the Texas Hill Country, traverses the Gulf States, and ends on the Florida coast—3,022 miles in all.

Seated in the ferry cafeteria next to Max and across the table from Benj—sipping a cup of the ersatz mocha that I'd made for myself using hot chocolate from a machine topped off with drip coffee—I couldn't hold back tears." Aunt Barb, remember how you took time off from college and went to Paris, where you didn't know anyone, didn't know French, and didn't have any money? And remember how when I took a break from school, you told me I could learn a lot about art by going to Paris? You practically shoved me onto the plane." He reached over and put his hand on mine. "I know this is hard, but I also know you have an inner adventurer that you can summon up for Max's trip."

"Maybe, Benj," I replied, "I'll try. Not sure I'll be successful, but I'll try."

I finished the mocha, and the three of us walked down to the car deck, where the guys had left their bikes. The bright pink handlebars gave Max's bike, a gift from Benj, a rakish air. Benj loved unexpected colors and styles. While in college, he'd dyed his hair bright green, and on his first date with the young woman who would become his wife, he'd worn multicolored bowling shoes. The bike was extremely well built, and I tried not to think about how the pink handlebars would go over in West Texas.

The California road was narrow and winding, climbing hundreds of feet through redwoods so dense that a sign advised drivers to turn on their lights. I broke into a sweat. Forty-five minutes earlier, Craig and I had driven past Max when he was on the side of the road, then wider and straighter, checking his map and taking huge gulps from his water bottle. He was now far behind us. My stomach lurched as enormous logging trucks sped by, almost squeezing us off the road. I searched for the shoulders on which Max would be riding, only to discover that on the hairiest of the curves, they had disappeared.

When we at last emerged from the redwoods, I sighed with relief. *Okay*, I thought, *that was bad, but hopefully the next part will be better*. I figured visibility would be clearer on the coast. We made a final turn, and the Pacific Ocean was once again on our right. But instead of the tranquil waters I'd anticipated, the ocean was churning, and the wind was so strong the car began to shake. Too worried to say more than "Holy shit!"—both of us gripped by morbid fantasies—Craig clutched the steering wheel, and I white-knuckled my seat. Finally, we arrived in Fort Bragg on the Mendocino coast and checked into the no-frills motel that we'd booked the night before because it was right off the bike route. When Craig told the woman at the front desk that we were meeting our son, who was bicycling in from Garberville, she shook her head, the creases in her forehead deepening. "We get a lot of cyclists through here," she said. "I always wonder if they know what they're up against in these mountains and along this stretch of the coast." She noted the horrified expression on my face and hastily added, "But I'm sure he'll be fine."

"We should drive back to meet him," I said. My heart was beating fast, and I thought I might pass out. "He can't possibly ride in that wind." I glanced out the window at trees bent from constant ocean winds and pulled on my jacket, ready to dart out of the office and into our parked car. And then, I saw Max on the other side of the window, his muscular legs easing his bike to a stop and a triumphant grin across his face. Relief coursed through my body. I held him close, shaking with the fear of what could have been.

"The ride was great," he announced. "The wind was with me, so I made really good time." Then he saw the concern in my eyes. "Yeah, I knew about the traffic and the climb, but I didn't tell you ahead of time so you wouldn't worry. I knew it would be especially hard for you, Mom."

I felt a jangled mix of emotions: fury that Kelsey had been killed, frustration with Adventure Cycling for recommending the route, and anger that Max had felt the need to take the trip at all. But I also felt a growing sense of pride. My strong and gentle son had completed a difficult ride with skill and courage. My eyes filled with tears, and I hugged him again.

It was hard to get to sleep that night. The word *dangerous* kept flashing in my head. *It's not normal to want to ride on a road with trucks zooming past*, I thought, *or on cliffs with a drop-off to the ocean, battling wind and rain. How will Max survive?* I fell asleep at last and had a dream in which Kelsey advised me to get rid of my *old, tired stencils* and find new ones. When I awoke, I realized that the *stencils* were my constant alertness to danger, and Kelsey was right: It was time to find new ones. But how?

Craig and I left Max in San Francisco and returned home. A friend rode with him for a few days in California, Benj joined him again for several days in West Texas, and another friend biked with him for a day outside of Austin—but mostly Max rode by himself. I accompanied him from home, following each segment of his journey on the set of maps I'd bought, avidly studying route elevations, riding conditions, and possible concerns along the way.

The Adventure Cycling Association continually revises its maps because of changes in the road and terrain in an unending attempt to find the widest shoulders, the smoothest roads, and the least vehicular traffic. Each of the seven maps for the southern cross-country route is divided into smaller segments that can be slipped into the pocket of a vest, with suggestions for where to camp, where to get your bike repaired, and what sights to see along the way. In many ways, the Adventure Cycling maps were like my attempts to map out the terrain of grief by giving myself plenty of space, surrounding myself with comfort, and avoiding situations that might trigger pain. But Max's bike trip demanded that I face my fears.

He texted us each morning to tell us his plans for the day and called or texted each evening to let us know where he'd stopped for the night. I checked the Weather Channel frequently, estimating the impact of wind and elevation on Max's riding speed, trying to determine when he would arrive at his planned destination for the day. I was worried about tornadoes and obsessively looked for information about approaching storms. One evening, Max said, "Mom, stop letting me know what the Weather Channel says about tornadoes. I can get local information." By the next evening, he'd changed his mind. "Actually, I think it's a good idea for you to check and let me know if you see a tornado coming." I didn't ask what had prompted him to change his mind.

My accompaniment to Max's journey was spiritual as well as physical, a silent and almost ceaseless prayer. Sometimes I pleaded with Kelsey: *I'm so worried about Max. I don't know if you can do anything to keep him safe, but if you can, please be with him*

throughout his trip.
  I'm with him, Mom, always.

Even though I tried to block morbid thoughts, to relax, and to see the trip through new stencils, again and again I came back to the possibility of losing another child. Eventually, as Max's trip neared the end—although I still followed the bicycle maps, checked the weather, and prayed unceasingly—I began to feel more certain that he'd finish the ride in one piece.

One afternoon, when Max was only a couple of days from his final destination, I was in Seattle, sorting through the mail, when my eyes were caught by a shiny catalog from an outdoor adventure company. I flopped down on the sofa and turned the pages with growing excitement. I flipped through the advertisements once again, mesmerized by photos of men, women, and children hiking in the mountains, camping alongside steams, and bicycling next to alpine meadows. The catalog felt like more than just a compendium of ads; it felt like a sacred text. But what was it telling me? Suddenly, I thought, *God loves adventure!* The sense of dread that had been weighing me down since Max started his trip lifted. That night, I dreamed of God hiking through mountains, ready for adventure, and the God in my dream was a woman. (When Kelsey was about three, she had insisted, "God is a woman, and her name is Africa.") My inner guide—*Kelsey?* —was telling me that it was time to open up to the world, time to regain my sense of adventure.

Max completed his trip, shipped his bike home, and flew back to Seattle, strong and resilient. "I'm glad I did it," he said, "but I don't think I'll ever want to go on a solo cross-country ride again." I asked him whether the journey had helped with his grief. "I think so. I still miss Kelsey but it's not such an ache."

I was proud of him, although my heart skipped a beat whenever he—or Sam—mentioned riding their bikes on busy Seattle streets. In those moments, I inhaled deeply and tried to breathe out my trepidation. That was an improvement, a new stencil.

In the spring of 2022, close to the tenth anniversary of Kelsey's death, my mood matched the gloominess of the rainy day. As I drove along the slick streets on my way to visit Mom in the memory care unit of her retirement center, memories of the past decade swirled around me like fog: moving Mom and Dad into the retirement facility, sitting next to Dad's body a year later, picking up Mom after learning of Kelsey's death, visiting her every week and noting her deepening dementia. Over the past decade, I had often taken Mom to lunch at one of the many restaurants near the center. The last time I took her out, she fretted the entire time, becoming more and more agitated. Her questions swamped my attempts to steer us into a pleasant conversation: "How long are we staying here?" "When will we go back?" "Do I have enough money?" She was far more at ease when I ate lunch with her in the dining room of her memory care unit.

As I entered the lounge of the memory care unit on that rainy morning, Mom—clad in an American flag T-shirt under a sweater that had become several sizes too big—was asleep in her wheelchair in front of the TV. A low-budget religious movie, *Acts of the Apostles*, was playing. I put my arm around her shoulders and whispered into her ear, "Hi, Mom."

Her eyes flew open, and she smiled. I don't know whether she remembered my name, but she knew I was someone she cared about. I rubbed her back and her arthritic hands and rested my head on her shoulder. I felt like a little girl again, my heart awash in love for my mama.

"Is it time?" she asked.

"*Time?*" I replied. "Time for what?"

She shrugged. She was losing weight, slept most of the time, and was halfway through her ninety-ninth year. Was she asking whether it was time to eat or time to die? She fell asleep, and quietly I put on my coat and left.

On the drive home, I passed a young woman who was walking along Route 99, wearing a scanty top and shorts despite the cold and rain. When she realized I was an older woman driving alone, she quickly turned back to her phone. My heart went out to her. It's a dangerous life for those who solicit along this stretch of the highway. I prayed, "May all sex workers be safe."

Farther on, I drove through a long tunnel and emerged to see a forest of cargo-loading cranes on my right, low warehouses on my left, and a large cement factory just ahead. I passed by Seattle's large

South Transfer Station and thought about my grandpa asking if we kids wanted to accompany him on a trip to the dump. Going to the dump was exciting because you never knew what you might find there. My brothers were always on the lookout for a baseball card that could be worth a fortune. I crossed a bridge and thought about the Duwamish, the original inhabitants of Seattle, whose sacred river flowed beneath me. The Duwamish River now teemed with toxic chemicals from plants such as Boeing. And I thought about the Seattle poet Richard Hugo, who grew up nearby and caught catfish and perch in the days when they were still plentiful in the not-yet-polluted waterway.

Eventually, I turned onto our tree-lined street in Seattle, the Salish Sea briefly visible, and pulled up in front of our house. *Had it been an adventure, this sometimes sad, sometimes gloomy morning?* The first definition of *adventure* in my dictionary is "an undertaking usually involving danger and unknown risks." That didn't fit, but the second definition, "an exciting or remarkable experience," seemed closer to the mark. I had a chance to hold my mom's hand, to be warmed by her smile, to put my head on her shoulder, and to feel like a little girl again. Despite the fury that the Buddhist loving kindness prayer had aroused in me during the early days of loss, I found myself praying it along my drive home—spontaneously and with my whole heart. Much of the scenery was industrial, not at all lovely, but I had taken pleasure in the journey. It seemed to me then that every moment *could* be remarkable. Every moment held the *possibility* of adventure.

chapter twenty-six
Weddings and
New Possibilities

"We are so happy to have you in our family, Annie. Kelsey would have loved you. I know because of how much I love you." Max, wearing a new suit, his hair cut for the occasion, raised his glass in a toast to his new sister-in-law. I gulped, trying unsuccessfully to staunch my tears, and looked around the repurposed ferry boat—polished oak floors, kerosene lamps, white flowers, and glowing candles—and noticed that everyone around me also had been touched by Max's words. It was 2015, three years after Kelsey died.

Sam and Annie were married in the church Craig had pastored for ten years, where he and I celebrated our wedding, and where all three of our kids were baptized. The church was built in the early twentieth century, and many facets of its architecture and decoration, such as the clinker brick facade, had been influenced by the Arts and Crafts movement. The long and narrow narthex with an arched ceiling opened to a sanctuary that was beautiful in its simplicity: cream-colored plaster walls, high oak beams, and large, arched windows that infused the space with sunlight even on a cloudy day.

A reader board next to the outside walkway proclaimed, *Come as you are. All are welcome.* When I started attending the church in the days before I became romantically involved with Craig, weekly AA groups met in the church parlor, and a gay square dance group used the fellowship hall for its regular gatherings. Several years later, the congregation declared themselves "open and affirming to people of all sexual orientations, gender identities, and gender expressions."

When I was pregnant with Kelsey—after a frustrating and often disappointing year and a half of trying to conceive—Craig included phrases like "pregnant with possibility" and "breathing new life into old" in his sermons, sharing our wonder and delight with the entire congregation. Kelsey was named for Frank Kelsey, who had been a close friend even before he and his wife joined the church.

When Kelsey was four and attending pre-school three days each week, two-year-old Sam and I often visited the church's homeless drop-in center. The unofficial host of the center was a Native American man named Art, who was in his mid to late thirties and living on the street. Art was over the moon when I walked in the door with a toddler and often sneaked Sam sugary treats, much to Sam's surprised delight since he wasn't allowed many such sweets at home. Art died on the street later that year, and Sam doesn't remember him. But I'm certain that Art and people like him, whom Sam met or heard about as he was growing up, kindled in him his deep-seated compassion for people on the margins of society.

Sam and Annie were acquainted in high school, but only as casual friends. It wasn't until they were in graduate school—Annie in medical school at the University of Washington and Sam getting his Master of Divinity degree at Pacific School of Religion in Berkeley—that their romance ignited. Annie, tall and slim with long dark brown hair, had been on the Under 19 National Team of USRowing and had rowed for Princeton. At the time of the wedding, she was a resident in Family Medicine in Seattle.

A couple of years before the wedding, Sam, Annie, Craig, and I adopted our dog Tucker from an animal shelter north of Seattle. Tucker spent half his time in their city apartment and the other half with us on Marrowstone. I thought at the time of the adoption, *I better do this dog-sharing right because it'll affect whether or not they trust me with future grandchildren.* By the time of the wedding, we had worked out all the kinks.

During the days after Kelsey's death, I said to Annie, "I don't know how I can get through the next day, let alone the rest of my life." She listened intently, squeezed my hand, and helped me get through the next day and the next and the next. She baked cookies when Sam's anguish was particularly acute or when he needed a pick me up, and he baked bread for all their special occasions. He nurtured her through medical school and residency; she encouraged him as he found his way to becoming both a clinical psychologist and an ordained minister.

A week or so before the wedding, I was at the church when Sam told the organist that he wanted the ceremony to include a couple of hymns. He was especially keen to sing a hymn with the refrain, "How can I keep from singing," to let everyone know that despite his sadness about losing Kelsey, he was overjoyed to be marrying Annie. The organist visibly blanched, realizing that the hymn also included a stanza about "prison cell and dungeon vile," and said, "I think the hymn will be great, but may I make a few modifications to the lyrics?" Sam agreed, and the amended hymn was perfect.

A year after Sam and Annie were married, Kelsey's close friend and college roommate Katie asked me to officiate at her wedding. She'd met Ben in Chicago a couple of years before when she moved from New York back to her hometown. When I met Ben, my first thought was, *I really like him*; my second was, *Kelsey would really like him, too*.

When Katie and Ben came to Marrowstone the spring before their summer wedding to plan the ceremony, we sat in Adirondack chairs on our back deck, looking out at the garden and the woods beyond, talking about what to include in the ceremony—and of course about Kelsey. When I was in bed later that night, I had one of my by-then-regular conversations with Kelsey:

What do you think of Ben? I asked her.

I can't imagine anyone better for Katie.

I know and I'm glad for her. But, as always, I wish you were here, sweet girl.

Since Katie is Jewish, they wanted to include seven blessings in their wedding, as is the custom in Judaism—but didn't want to use the traditional blessings. They viewed each of the ways in which family members and friends were participating in the ceremony as a blessing. Holding the huppah, welcoming the guests, remembering deceased family members and friends, lighting the candles, reciting a poem, reading a prayer, playing music.

At one point during the wedding, Katie tapped me on the shoulder and said. "You promised to dance at my wedding, so come dance with me." I was touched that she remembered and put down my glass of champagne to join her on the dance floor. As I looked around at the laughing young people, my throat tightened: Kelsey should have been there.

Hey, Mom, you keep forgetting. I am here, especially today. I'm here with you and with all my friends.

Max and Alexandra were married three years later. Their romance began soon after they graduated from high school, and they stayed together until midway through college. I'm not sure when their love affair resumed, but the first Craig and I knew about it was during Max's bicycle trip. He used an extra day of his usually very tight schedule to spend time in Los Angeles with Alexandra, who was finishing graduate school. Once she'd completed her master's in social work and moved back to Seattle, their relationship deepened. The look on Max's face when he gazed at Alexandra made me realize that even though he had dated other women during the years they were apart, there really never had been anyone else for him.

Alexandra, with curly black hair and freckles, is half Kenyan and half European American; she was raised by her single mom who died of cancer a year before Max's bike trip. Although Alexandra had been known as *Alex* for most of her life, after her mom died, she asked to be called by the name her mother always used for her. I loved getting to know Alexandra—from the young confident woman she was when Max and she were first dating to the more mature but still self-assured and sensitive woman she had become—and I was grateful for our easygoing yet continually expanding relationship.

Max and Alexandra were married in August 2019, on a hillside estate south of Seattle, underneath an arbor with late-blooming wisteria. The weather was warm and sunny, with no smoke from wildfires as in recent years. Sam was best man and Benj the officiant. Max and Alexandra wrote their own vows, mentioning concepts that were relevant to their lives such as *white privilege* and *intersectionality.* As a mixed-race couple, they were determined to support each other and raise their children with mindfulness in a world plagued by persistent racism.

The reception was held under an awning beneath a clear, starlit sky. At all the other weddings I'd been to since Kelsey's death, I had danced in an attempt to turn my mourning into dancing, but at Max and Alexandra's wedding, seven years after Kelsey died, my joy far outweighed my sadness. I danced to songs I knew well and to songs I'd never heard before—and through it all, I felt Kelsey's presence.

What do you think of my dancing, Kelsey? My moves are any-thing but cool—but I'm giving it my all.

Looks like you're really having fun, and I love seeing Max and Alexandra so happy.

There is a way of mending broken pots—called kintsugi in Jap-anese—in which the chards are rejoined using lacquer mixed with gold or silver: What was shattered becomes whole again, rendered into a vessel that is more interesting and even more beautiful than before. So too can it be with people. Although vestiges of sadness and pain persist in those who have lost a loved one, transformation into a new kind of wholeness can bring unexpected gifts and beauty. Kintsugi was becoming a metaphor for my life, and the three wed-dings of my beloveds were a part of *my* transformation.

chapter twenty-seven
Journeying

I was ready to learn how to journey. I'd been visited by the spirits of mothers who'd lost children to the sea, received comfort from owls on the island, from rocks on the beach, and from a single maple leaf that waved to me each morning. I'd been guided by salmon and ravens in British Columbia and studied mystical texts from several religions. The refrain "Don't limit God" kept playing in my head.

After we'd lived on Marrowstone for several years, Craig and I became part of a small drumming circle there. Four of us—Linda, Mark, Craig, and I—met once a week in each couple's homes. Linda, with twinkling eyes behind green-rimmed glasses and an energy that belied her graying hair, was an experienced shamanic practitioner who taught Craig and me how to use the steady beat of our drums to journey beyond ordinary reality to the world of spirit. Her husband, Mark, now retired from a career as a health care administrator and fit from long hours of working outdoors, had been drumming with Linda for years. Craig and I were the neophytes.

Craig's drum, as large as a knight's shield and made from leather stretched over polished wood, has a design of Celtic knots around the rim. The drum doesn't resonate when cold, and Craig has to warm it in front of a stove or fire. Mine is smaller, made of synthetic material, and doesn't lose its timbre because of temperature fluctuations.

Before drumming, we light a candle and set an intention for the journey, usually inspired by what's happening in our own lives or in the news. The pace of our drumming is twice the rate of a normal heartbeat, and the rhythm is steady without syncopation. I hold my drum in my left hand and my drum beater in my right. My shoulders and arms sometime ache from the rapid pace of the drumming, but my pain mostly is forgotten by the middle of a journey. As the drumming intensifies and the timbre changes from a light to a thunderous reverberation, I bend my body closer to my drum. If I have journeyed to a special place—amid a gathering of wise women, for example, or near the center of the Milky Way—I drum loudly and with more exuberance, sometimes thinking, *I could stay here forever.* Linda had warned Craig and me of the danger of staying in an alternate reality, so I'm always mindful of the need to return to the ordinary world.

If an animal pops into mind and accompanies someone for much of a journey, it may be considered a spirit guide—a concept deriving from shamanic practices throughout the world and especially from Native American spirituality. My first guide was a lion that stayed with me for several journeys, but soon other animals showed up. Over the years, Raven, Salmon, and Eagle have been my most frequent spirit guides—no surprise given my experience in the Great Bear Rainforest—and occasionally I'm guided by a very wise worm.

Shamanism is a way of connecting with the spiritual nature of all of creation. While on a shamanic journey, one travels to alternate realities, often labeled as the *lower*, *middle*, and *upper worlds*. In the lower world where I begin my journey, I imagine a path next to a meandering creek that eventually curves to the right and opens to a meadow. The middle world is the spiritual aspect of the earthly world. I sometimes journey to a place I know well, such as the mouth of Chimacum Creek or to a place that holds power, such as Wall Street or Washington, D.C. The upper world is where one meets the spirits of those who have died. I often talk with Kelsey, although I'm usually afraid to stay with her for very long, maybe reluctant to outstay my welcome, maybe because the connection seems too good to be true, or maybe because I might never leave.

Shamanism is probably the oldest of all spiritual practices and has been observed for thousands of years. My Viking ancestors venerated female shamans called *volür* who walked from estate to estate providing guidance and healing. I like knowing that my new spiritual practice is linked to a practice followed by my ancestors. But of course, it's only one among a multitude of spiritual paths. U.S. theologian Matthew Fox writes in his book *One River, Many Wells: Wisdom Springing From Global Faiths* that we get into trouble, as a religion and as a people, when we mistake the well for the river. I seem to be drinking from a variety of wells: I love ancient Jewish texts, Christian and Islamic mystical writings, Quaker silence, and shamanic drumming. In some ways, a shamanic journey is like writing Midrash: creating new interpretations and new worlds in the blank spaces—imagination in the service of Spirit.

During a period of time when I was especially beset by doubts about whether my regular conversations with Kelsey were nothing more than wishful thinking, an experienced shaman whom my drumming friend Linda knew and respected, journeyed to the upper world on my behalf and sent an email message to me: "Kelsey is fine. I'm not a medium, so I don't usually bring messages, but she asked me to let you know that she has been sending you signs for a long time and wonders why you haven't been recognizing them. She'll start sending them again."

Certainly, I'd had doubts over the years since Kelsey died: *Did she really speak to me in my dreams? Did I imagine her presence? Were the messages from ravens and owls real or imagined? Was I only imagining our conversations?*

I went into a state of alert, watching for new messages from Kelsey. When someone in our Quaker meeting said something that touched me deeply, I wondered, *Is this a sign?* When a raven flew over Tucker and me as we were walking along the road. *A message?* When a sunrise was particularly spectacular. When a book seemed to leap off the library shelf. When a bee stayed with me at a safe distance for an inordinate amount of time. Indications of spirit were everywhere, but were they the promised messages from Kelsey? Then I had a couple of dreams that jolted me. In the first one, I had a vivid conversation with her:

Kelsey: I told you that I was in your life. Why do you have so much difficulty believing it?

Me: Because if I discover it isn't true, then I'll lose you all over again.

When I awoke, my heart felt light. *I'd been with Kelsey!* And then, the import of our conversation hit me: *I'm afraid of losing her again.* I inhaled deeply. *Yes, it's true*, I thought. *That's why I have trouble believing.*

In the second dream, Kelsey spoke to me again: *Mom, I'm waiting for you at home.* I awoke thinking, *I don't have to go looking for her. She's right here.* I suppose the words of the dream could have meant that Kelsey was waiting for me in some kind of after life, but that's not how it felt; rather, she seemed to be reaffirming her presence in my life. *Home* meant that Kelsey was with me wherever I was. The word *home* became a mantra for my meditations and prayers.

A few days after I received the message from the shaman, our small drumming circle journeyed for spiritual guidance on how to be more trusting of signs and messages. As the four of us closed our eyes and began to drum, I imagined walking to my favorite tree and descending through it into the lower world. There I met Eagle, who carried me to the middle world and to the spirit of the sun. When I asked how I could become more trusting of messages from Kelsey, I received this response: *Remember how your body feels when you lie on a driftwood log on the first sunny day of spring and allow the warmth to soak into every pore? Whenever you think something might be a sign or message, notice how you feel: If a waving maple leaf eases your heartache, you can trust it's a sign. If a sense of presence gives you goosebumps, you can believe it's real. Too often your brain overrules your senses. You need to practice trusting.*

On another journey, we traveled to the spirit of *Alnilam*, the middle star of Orion's belt. When I was getting ready to leave, I asked if I could learn *star language*. Alnilam responded, *Of course! And the best teacher is your grandson, Willie.*

Our grandson, Willie—Sam's and Annie's son—had been teaching me star language since his birth in the summer of 2018. As a tiny baby, he looked into my eyes with such trust that my heart melted. At three, he loved cars, trucks, trains—and flowers. He could tell me the names of every construction vehicle—backhoe, excavator, compactor, front loader, and crane to name a few—and the name for many of the flowering plants grown in the Pacific Northwest. On a drive from his house to ours, he asked me to maneuver close to the trucks parked along the road so he could take pictures of them with his small toy camera. When we got to our house, he wanted to photograph flowers. "Let's go on whatever walk has the most beautiful flowers," he announced as he jumped from the car to the sidewalk in front of our house. Because it was spring, we took a walk around the block and found gorgeous flowers in every yard. Willie was ecstatic. "Oh look, a rhododendron! And there's a Japanese maple!" He saw pink heather and ran toward it with squeals of delight.

Much of our time together that spring when he was three was spent digging in the dirt. I added amendments to the soil, and he shoveled dirt and sometimes fertilizers into a large blue pot, making a "yucky stew." He told his parents that the highlight of his day was when I gave him chicken manure to put into the stew. I derive so much more joy from being with Willie—and now Willie's sister, Lila, and Max and Alexandra's daughter, Amaya—than I thought possible. When I'm with them, I live in the moment: star language.

On the drive from our sons' houses to ours—they both live relatively close to us—Craig and I pass an alley that for some reason was named *Kelsey Lane*. The first time I saw the street sign, on our way to view the house we eventually bought, I thought of it as an omen. In fact, in many ways it seemed like Kelsey was guiding Craig and me to that house. We'd been looking at condos and houses for sale in Seattle for months, but nothing seemed quite right. Within the first ten minutes of being in the house in West Seattle, we were ready to make an offer, and three days later it was accepted at a lower price than we'd anticipated in the hot real estate market. It all went so smoothly and so quickly that it astonished not only us but also our realtor, our friends, and our kids. Willie often points out Kelsey Lane to me. "There it is, Bee—there's Kelsey Lane," he says. We've been in the house for over a year, and since it still makes my heart sing, I'm trusting that it's a sign from Kelsey that we're home at last.

chapter twenty-eight
Chimacum Creek

As I eased myself onto a weathered driftwood log at the mouth of Chimacum Creek, close to Marrowstone Island but on the mainland, it began to rain, a few drops, not much. It was low tide, and the creek was a narrow rivulet slowly making its way to the sea. At high tide it's more like a river, an amalgam of fresh water and salt water. Across the creek, swirls of red madrona weaved through a blanket of evergreens. Gulls swooped to snatch bits of shellfish on the beach, and herons watched for passing minnows in the gently curling waves close to shore. I took a deep breath, the air pungent with the aroma of seaweed and fish.

Our dog, Tucker, stood at the edge of the creek, glugging water. Flavored by algae, fish, and God knows what else, that water must have seemed to him like drinking fine wine—so much better than the water at home. He raised his head and sniffed, alert for signs of a river otter, then dipped his mouth into the icy water again, huffing when algae caught in his throat. Soon after we'd adopted Tucker, Sam commented, "Tucker has a drinking problem." The sound of his drinking, no matter whether in our kitchen or at the creek, is extremely loud, but it always makes me smile.

Tucker has only one eye—his other was shot by a BB gun long before we adopted him—giving me an advantage whenever a river otter is making its way down the creek or frolicking in the sea. Since the range of Tucker's vision is limited, I often see the otter before he does, which allows me just enough time to snap on his leash. Once, when my attention was on the beach rather than the creek, Tucker was in the water before I could stop him and quickly paddled literally within striking distance of an otter, receiving a gash on his leg—fortunately not too deep. It gives me such pleasure to watch Tucker run, climb, and dart in and out of waves, that most of the time I let him run free, counting on my vigilance to keep him and the sea creatures safe. We got Tucker a year after Kelsey's death, and no matter how unhappy I've been, he has always lifted my spirit. I'm not quite sure why Tucker is such a great source of healing—maybe because he's the embodiment of living fully and joyfully in the present.

I saw an eagle overhead and searched the treetops for its mate. Oftentimes, when I see an eagle flying overhead or perched on the limb of a tree, I sing a variation of the hymn "On Eagle's Wings" that was part of the memorial service Boston College held for Kelsey. I sing it more than once, like a chant, loving the *eagle's wings* metaphor for what I imagine to be Kelsey's after-life journey.

A great blue heron, one of the pair that lived in the trees near the creek, was heading to its favorite perch in a fir. The previous fall, there had been twelve herons at the mouth of the creek each morning, waiting for the fingerling chum to make their way downstream. I tried to imitate the bending and arching of a heron's graceful neck as it seizes and then swallows a fish. Advanced practitioners of shamanism have learned to shape-shift, which means they *become* a different life form—a tree, an animal, or maybe even a rock. Once our drumming friends, Linda and Mark, were walking in the state park on Marrowstone with a friend of theirs who was an accomplished shamanic practitioner. When the three of them saw a cougar about to pounce on a doe, Linda and Mark's friend shape-shifted into another deer, confusing the cougar. The doe passed by unharmed. I wasn't trying to shape-shift—that certainly was beyond my ability—but I wanted to get an idea of how the heron might feel as it bent its long and graceful neck. I liked getting at least somewhat out of my own body. I couldn't shape-shift, but I could imagine doing so.

The beach faces Indian Island, once the home of the S'Klallam chief, Chetzemoka, but since the middle of the twentieth century, a U.S. Navy base. I gazed at the slender metal crane that loads deadly arsenal into warships, and below it, the steel-gray ship waiting to be stocked. In the early days of grief, I avoided views of the navy crane, unable to accept a complexity that included both the crane and the beauty that surrounded it.

For quite a while following the trauma of Kelsey's death, I found it hard to accept spiritual uncertainty. Craig and I were walking on the beach a month or so after she died when I asked him to tell me how he saw the relationship between God and Kelsey. I wanted him to diagram it on the beach. He obliged by drawing a large circle in the sand with his foot. "Let's say this is God," he said. He drew another circle inside the first, but with just about the same diameter. "And let's say this is Kelsey."

"But they're the same!" I exclaimed. "I want to know where God ends and where Kelsey begins."

"I don't know if there's a difference."

Even though I was beginning to sense that there wasn't a firm boundary between Kelsey and God, in the days and weeks after Kelsey's death, I found metaphysical ambiguities both perplexing and terrifying. Questions—like *Where does God end, and Kelsey begin?*—went round and round in my head.

Much of the beach was covered by a dusting of finely ground white shells, likely the remains of a midden, or refuse heap, for the Chimacum people who had tossed their shells on that very beach for thousands of years. The entire Chimacum village was wiped out in a mid-nineteenth-century massacre, leaving their midden as the only evidence of the village's former existence. When I first started walking along the beach, pulled by a force I didn't understand, I googled *Chimacum* and found conflicting reports as to who had attacked and why. It seemed likely, however, that neighboring tribes had united for the assault. According to most sources, the Chimacum were universally hated because of their bellicose disposition—but the presence I felt didn't seem malevolent. Quite the contrary. I sensed harmony. *How could that be, given the stories?* I wondered.

I once met a person with Chimacum heritage, and she shared with me another possibility: There had been a massacre, not because the Chimacum wanted war but simply because they didn't speak the same language or share the culture of neighboring tribes. As I listened to this woman talk about her ancestors, I sensed multiple time periods coming together in the present moment, an intuition that had I had been experiencing more and more frequently since Kelsey's death.

Hey, Kelsey. I feel the presence of the Chimacum people who once lived on this beach—but I'm wondering if I'm just imagining it.

You use your imagination for drumming journeys and for our conversations, so why not now?

You're right. I love what Joan of Arc said to the interrogators at her trial who accused her of imagining her call from God: "How else would God speak to me, if not through my imagination?"

Those words should be etched on your heart, Mom.

I moved from the beach to the grassy knoll where a historic marker described the ironworks that occupied the site in the late nineteenth and early twentieth centuries. The small town that surrounded the ironworks included a one-cell jail. The layers of complexity astounded me, and I no longer shied away from it—what a change from my early days of grief.

My eyes were drawn to another eagle, flying quickly as if on a mission. It landed on the branch of a fir near where the jail once stood. On the same branch but almost hidden, was its mate. The eagles seemed to be a message from Kelsey, an indication that she was present. A chant burst into my mind, and I sang it over and over: "Kelsey is closer than my breath, nearer than my heart." Since only the eagles and Tucker were around to hear, I chanted louder with each repetition. The universe seemed larger and more intricate than ever before, and yet Kelsey was closer than my breath.

chapter twenty-nine
Companioning

"It's early days for you," said Robin, a few minutes into our first meeting during the fall of 2012. She sipped her latte, pushed a strand of gray-blond hair from her eyes, and looked at me with concern. "It's only been three months since Kelsey died. It'll get better."

"I know I won't 'get over' her death, but I don't want it to be all I think about."

"I know what you mean. It can get kind of boring, can't it? Not your love for Kelsey, but the feelings that repeat themselves again and again."

"It's *so* boring!"

We laughed. It felt astonishingly wonderful to laugh with someone who *understood*. A mutual friend had suggested we meet, because she thought it might be helpful for me to talk with someone more experienced with grief than I was. Robin's twenty-year-old son had died a couple of years before Kelsey. As soon as I met Robin, I could tell by her lively face and sparkling eyes that she was once again enjoying life—which gave me more hope than reading a score of books. We met every month or so for coffee and took long walks through the Bainbridge Island town of Winslow where she lived—a forty-five-minute drive from our Marrowstone home. We often laughed in the ways you can do only when you have shared a difficult experience. Who could I do that with except someone who had lost a child?

A few years after the death of her son, Robin became a grief counselor, meeting with people individually and running grief groups. Eventually, she and a retired psychiatrist, well-versed in death and dying, founded Compassionate Companions, a program that provides support and companionship for the bereaved. Robin and her colleague recruit volunteers who have experienced a significant loss and coach them to listen, support, and be open to the many and varied ways people grieve. I became a companion and was matched with a woman in her fifties whose twenty-year-old son had died from an undiagnosed heart condition. She lived about sixty miles from Marrowstone, so we met for lunch each month in Port Gamble, a town halfway between our homes, in a small café that overlooked the Salish Sea, talking, often crying, and sometimes exploding in laughter over something seemingly dark but also humorous that one of us had said. I also met with a young woman whose mother had recently died. I'd been paired with her, according to Robin, because both of us were interested in talking about the spiritual dimensions of loss.

There were other grieving mothers with whom I corresponded over the years, although not through a structured program. A year after Kelsey died, Benj asked if I'd be willing to talk with the mother of one of his coworkers who'd died by suicide. The mother lived in Wisconsin, so meeting in person was never really an option, but we had frequent phone conversations. She expressed an eagerness to get on with the healing that surprised me. After Kelsey's death, I couldn't talk to anyone outside my family and closest friends for many weeks, but here she was, just two weeks after her daughter's death, on the phone with a stranger and ready to do whatever it took to begin healing. I tentatively suggested a book on grief, and the next time we talked she said, "Once I hung up from our conversation, I bought the book and read it in one sitting. Do you have another title to suggest?" She was a kindred spirit, finding solace in books. We began calling and emailing back and forth, sharing books and our impressions of each of them. I never met her or her husband in person, but they both wrote to tell me how important I'd been to them at a very difficult time. Not so long ago, I accidentally called her via FaceTime and was thrilled to see her face. She looked a bit like I'd expected although maybe younger: with brown hair, glasses, and wearing a plaid flannel shirt and a big smile.

A friend told me, shortly after Kelsey died, that it took her a very long time to move through intense grief following her husband's death, but she felt, almost from the beginning, a powerful empathy for anyone struggling with a similar loss and an intense desire to help in any way possible. It required a year or so for me to sufficiently move beyond the initial heartbreak to get to that same place, but I share her sentiment. A few years ago, someone I knew from when our kids were young unexpectedly lost her son. I dreamed about her, thought about her often, and tried to discern how best to help. For several months, I sent her occasional emails, assuring her I didn't need or expect a response. From time to time, she answered, telling me that something I'd said was just what she needed to hear. We never met in person other than at the memorial service—it never seemed to be something she wanted to do—but I continued to send emails and sometimes cards whenever prompted by my inner guide. Those promptings have since ceased, and I trust that my friend is finding the kind of support she needs. By now, she probably is giving support to others. I hope so.

During the initial, horrible days of my grief, our former neighbor and close friend Pam told me about an ancient Jewish tradition of granting a year of amnesty for anyone who has lost a spouse or a child: Nothing the grieving person says or does, including murder, can be held against them. Whether or not it was true, I loved the concept and granted myself a year of amnesty. I wasn't planning on killing anyone, but neither was I going to worry about unintentionally hurting someone's feelings. Since then, I've passed along to others the concept of grief amnesty. It's always been received with humor—and a sense of relief.

As I was preparing for Kelsey's memorial service, I sorted through boxes of family photographs so I could make an album for the reception. It was immensely painful to look at photographs of Kelsey, and yet I wanted others to see the laughing, joyful baby-child-woman whom we so dearly love. I began to say to myself, *I'm so grateful I was able to give birth to her. I'm so grateful I was able to braid her hair when she was young. I'm so grateful I was able to spend summers with her.* And the most powerful affirmation of all: *I'm so grateful I was given the opportunity to be Kelsey's mom.* The words of gratitude kept me from sinking into despair then—and they still do.

What is it about gratitude that's so powerful? I wondered. I'd been taught to say "thank you" for gifts or services, but the words I used while preparing the photo album went far beyond that, reminding me that Kelsey's life was more important than her death, that I wouldn't change a moment of our twenty-eight years together on earth. Although my heart was too broken to hold feelings of gratitude for more than a few seconds, the *words* of gratitude, were a form of prayer: *Please help me feel the gratitude that I know is there somewhere.* When eventually that prayer was answered, the gratitude that spilled over from my love for Kelsey included what was most important in life: love, kindness, generosity, and forgiveness,. In a kind of breathtaking alchemy, gratitude bred more gratitude until it became all-encompassing and ceaseless. Even though, at times, I've let clouds of doubt, despair, or anger obscure my gratitude, it's always there, summoning me to my better self.

The companioning hasn't stopped. Not long ago, I discovered that our new neighbors lost their twenty-year-old son in an automobile accident the same summer Kelsey died. I'd gone to a party at their home a week before and walked on the beach with the husband only the day before, but neither they nor I shared the most important fact of our lives—that we'd lost a child. It had been a decade since both of our children died, and it was no longer the first thing out of our mouths. Nevertheless, when I learned of their loss I rushed over to their house, and we spent the next hour talking about our children and about our journeys through heartache. There really is no one who understands the depth, the weight, and the contours of losing a child like another bereaved parent. I think of this excerpt from German-born American poet Lisel Mueller's "The Blind Leading the Blind":

> *Take my hand. There are two of us in this cave.*
> *The sound you hear is water; you will hear it forever.*
> *The ground you walk on is rock. I have been here before.*

When we support one another through grief, even though aspects of our pain and sorrow will last forever, by being together we can more easily discover the rock-solid ground beneath our feet.

chapter thirty
Ashes

We arrived at the beach around eight in the morning, just as the marine layer burned off to reveal sunshine and a cloudless blue sky. No one was around. Usually by then, there were a few people walking along the paths or on the beach with their dogs. Tucker leaped out of the back of the car, and I grabbed the navy-blue Eddie Bauer backpack containing the last of Kelsey's ashes. Craig and I had decided that the seventh anniversary of her death—June 1, 2019—was the right time to disperse them. A few years before, Sam, Annie, and Max had spent a weekend on Marrowstone to help Craig and me scatter most of her ashes, spreading them underneath eight rhododendrons, two tall dogwoods, a cascading willow below the garden, and the broadleaf maple with the leaf that had waved to me throughout the summer following her death. We'd saved a small amount of her ashes to scatter in the sea.

The seventh anniversary seemed especially important. I'd heard from others that it would take a long time until I could fully resume living, and the number *seven* stuck in my mind. I'm not sure why. Maybe because I read in a memoir about grief that it had taken the author seven years to fully reengage in life after her son's death. Maybe because Sally died at age seven. Maybe because in numerology, *seven* represents completeness. I do know that the early days of grieving felt like imprisonment, and I wanted to know the length of my sentence. Seven years seemed right.

As Craig, Tucker, and I slowly made our way down the beach toward the creek, two Canada geese swam close to the shore to greet us. Four great blue herons stood like sentinels, keeping watch over the mouth of the creek. As we walked around the cascading rocks that formed a partial boundary between the inlet and the sea, a bald eagle on the other side began a loud chirping. When we stopped, the eagle fell silent. "I guess this is where we're supposed to place the ashes," Craig said.

I put the backpack on a driftwood log and took out the bag of ashes. I could feel my heart pounding and tears building in my eyes as I reminded myself: *Kelsey is elsewhere, not in these ashes.* I opened the bag and emptied the contents into the water. Craig said quietly, "We love you, Kelsey."

The ashes rested briefly on top of the iridescent seawater before sinking. Just then, the eagle left its perch and flew to within a couple of feet of us, only inches above the ashes, tilting its wings in salute before flying fifty or so yards up the creek and landing on a high branch. "Wow! Can you believe *that*?" I said to Craig.

He shook his head, and we wrapped our arms around each other. Kelsey seemed near, the world around us replete with wonder. As we called to Tucker and picked up the backpack, the eagle flew back and landed on a fir across from us, the same one it had been perched on when we'd arrived. The eagle—representative of the many eagles I'd envisioned carrying Kelsey's spirit to heaven—seemed to be reassuring us that her ashes were now cared for by the planet. I had needed the past seven years to fully accept that Kelsey's earthly body belonged to the planet.

Not so long ago, I was trying to figure out the formula for my relationship to Kelsey. There were huge assumptions in my logic, but this is what I came up with:

If God = Kelsey and if God = me,
then Kelsey = me.
And if God = all that is on the planet and if God = Kelsey,
then all that is on the planet = Kelsey.

My formulas didn't lead to a proof of Kelsey's continuing existence, but they were comforting and expressed what I sensed in my heart: *I am one with Kelsey, Kelsey is one with the eagles. When I'm singing to an eagle, I'm singing to Kelsey. When an eagle soars above me, it's Kelsey who's lifting my spirits.*

My understanding of life—and of death—is enriched by the story of the universe that began over thirteen billion years ago with the explosion of an infinitesimal dot. Recent information gleaned through photographs taken by the James Webb Space Telescope call into doubt a well-accepted theory about the early formation of the universe: Apparently, the universe expanded much more quickly than astrophysicists had thought. That made me wonder: *What other theories will we have to revise as data continue to arrive? What if we discover that there was nothing before the infinitesimal dot? What if something can, indeed, come from nothing?* If it turns out that there is no transcendent creator, will we then turn to the poets and mystics rather than the theologians? Not so farfetched! Poets have been helping *me* make sense of my shattered inner world. Certainly, they can help me and probably many others make sense of a shattered cosmology—and a plethora of destroyed theologies. The following excerpt is from Walt Whitman's "O Me! O Life":

> *The question, O me! so sad, recurring—What good*
> *Amid these, O me, O life?*
>
> *Answer.*
> *That you are here—that life exists and identity,*
> *That the powerful play goes on, and you may*
> *Contribute a verse.*

I no longer need proof of the "power that made the universe"—or proof of Kelsey's continuing presence. I may have arrived at a point of accepting the mystery that surrounds both life and death. But of course, I still employ the qualifier, "may," and I'm not so sure there *is* a point of arrival. Yet I've come to believe I'm close.

chapter thirty-one
Women of Wisdom: The Grandmothers

I felt a distinct uneasiness, like something continuously slipping out of my grasp. I thought that my disquiet might come from trying to figure out where we would live when we could no longer care for our Marrowstone house and surrounding land. I felt a pit in my stomach when I thought of leaving the island: I'd miss preparing my garden each spring. I'd miss welcoming the bees, harvesting the peas and kale, watching for the first sign of tiny fruit amid the grape leaves. I'd miss my early-morning beach walks with Tucker and the pair of owls that call to each other at night.

We knew that we wouldn't always be able to maintain our Marrowstone way of life—and we wanted to live near our three grandchildren. That meant moving to Seattle. Was it the thought of leaving our island home that made me feel off-balance, left my nerves on edge? I wasn't sure, but the low buzzing in my head was getting stronger, more insistent, and it seemed to be saying: *Pay attention!*

Sam and Annie were expecting another child—a boy—in late spring of 2020, a month or so before Willie's second birthday. I'd always wanted more grandchildren but wondered if I could love another grandchild as much as I loved Willie. Was that the source of my uneasiness? Was that the crux my ever-present sorrow or was it something related? I would never be able to experience Kelsey becoming a mother. I would never be a grandmother to my daughter's child. There was something special about being the mother of the mother of a beloved grandchild, a unique bond that I would never have.

I'd often begun my daily meditation by reciting the chain of maternal family names, going back seven generations: Kelsey, daughter of Barbara, daughter of Eleanor, daughter of Emma, daughter of Gustafva, daughter of Anna Katarina, daughter of Maria. But since my *dis-ease* seemed to have something to do with being a grandmother, I made a shift in the recitation: Maria is grandmother to Gustafva, Anna Katarina is grandmother to Emma, Gustafva is grandmother to Eleanor, Emma is grandmother to Barbara, Eleanor is grandmother to Kelsey, Barbara is grandmother to Willie and his soon-to-arrive brother.

My breath caught in my throat—the matrilineal chain had been broken with Kelsey's death—but something besides a feeling of loss was stirring. I knew, of course, that I was Willie's grandmother, but suddenly I realized that I was one of *the grandmothers*, the women charged with passing on wisdom to succeeding generations, not dependent on having raised children or grandchildren but on sharing wisdom gained over a lifetime. The low buzzing in my head was gone, replaced by an awesome sense of responsibility.

I grew up with only one living grandmother, my dad's mother whom we first called Mama B and then shortened to B. For some reason, we grandchildren gave the name an entomological connection: *Bee*. I've called my grandmother "Bee" for most of my life. Whenever I do, a split-second image of flowers and honey flashes through my brain.

Shortly before the second world war, my grandparents moved from their home outside Chicago to a farm in central Illinois that my grandmother had inherited from her father. Bee grew a large vegetable garden, Papa raised cows and chickens, and a neighbor farmed the fields of corn. When Bee and Papa could no longer manage the garden and animals, they moved to a nearby town—forty miles from my childhood home.

Bee had a passion for fishing. I remember being about ten or eleven, sitting on the bank of Twin Lakes outside Paris, Illinois, next to a bucket of worms. "Just reach in the bucket and get a worm to put on your hook. Like this," Bee said, demonstrating the task with one easy motion.

I peered at the squirming mass of worms on the bottom of the bucket. "I can't!" I said, wrinkling my nose.

"Oh, for heaven's sake. I'll do it." Bee skewered a worm on my pole and told me to toss in my line.

During the summers of our growing-up years, Bee took us to the

Edgar County Fair outside of Paris. She loved harness racing: single horses, each pulling a light, two-wheeled cart. Six or seven of us grandchildren sat in the stands, dripping sweat from the sun beating down on us, waiting for the race to begin. Bee rummaged in her large, black pocketbook and found a quarter for each of us. "Put your money in a pile right here," she instructed, pointing to a spot next to her. "Whoever chooses the winning horse will win all the quarters." Suddenly, watching the harness race became a thrilling, high-stakes venture.

Bee and Papa showed up at our house every couple of weeks with Bee behind the wheel, honking the horn of their enormous Pontiac as she pulled into the driveway. The backseat was filled with food: enormous blocks of Colby cheese, vegetables from Bee's garden, an apple pie, and a box of sugar cookies. "Yoo-hoo, anybody home?" Bee walked through the front door with her pocketbook over one arm and a pie in the other, and Papa followed a few steps behind, carefully balancing the box of sugar cookies.

A couple of months after Kelsey died, I was driving to pick up Craig at the Kingston ferry landing and feeling miserable, when suddenly Bee was with me. I could *almost* smell her rose-scented powder, *almost* feel her arms around me. Although she didn't say a word, her love flowed through me like a river, and *that* I definitely felt. It was such an intense experience that I pulled off the road until I could stop shaking. I tried to phone Tricia, but there was no answer. *Maybe it's just as well,* I thought. *This is crazy stuff.* But crazy or not, the experience lifted me, for the moment, out of my gloom and brought Heaven a bit closer.

I don't know much about my maternal grandmother, Emma, who died when my mom was twelve, although I recently read a diary she kept while teaching in a one-room schoolhouse about thirty miles from her family's Iowa farm. She wasn't particularly enthusiastic about teaching, but she adored being picked up by her father in his horse-drawn cart to spend weekends with her family and attend the Saturday dances, game nights, and musical gatherings of their close-knit Swedish-American community.

A few years ago, I wanted to learn more about my great-grandmother Gustafva, who had immigrated from Sweden in 1879. Mom suggested that her cousin Beverly might know "something about my grandmother that I don't," and she handed me Beverly's telephone number. A couple of days later, Beverly told me on the phone, "Grandma never talked about Sweden, where she lived for the first twenty-four years of her life, except for two things: Her stepmother was mean, and she walked by herself to catch the boat to America."

Although Beverly didn't know *why* Gustafva thought of her stepmother as mean—and I could only speculate—I got goosebumps when I learned that she had walked over a hundred miles by herself from the family farm in Dalsland, Sweden, to Göteborg. I did some research and discovered that the manifest of the ship that carried her to New York records her as a "male tailor." Maybe it was a mistake, but I fantasized, not without reason, that she'd dressed as a man to ensure her safety during the long walk and subsequent voyage. The thought made me smile.

On a trip to Sweden a few years after Kelsey died, Craig and I found the road Gustafva walked to catch her boat. White birches and Norwegian spruce covered the hillside, and a blue lake shimmered in the afternoon sun. I closed my eyes and breathed in air that smelled of both woods and soil. The road is part of an ancient pilgrimage trail that heads north to the shrine of St. Olav in Trondheim and south to Göteborg, eventually joining other trails that feed into the Camino de Santiago, which spans five hundred miles from France through Spain. I considered Gustafva's long walk a pilgrimage and thought of Gustafva—who lost four children, three of them in childhood—as my companion through the joys and sorrows of life.

I'm now one of the host of grandmothers on both sides of the veil, charged with watching over and guiding future generations—a challenge that I don't take lightly. Nevertheless, since I have a long line of grandmothers supporting me, I trust I'll be fine.

chapter thirty-two
Avery

A month before our second grandson's due date, Sam called to tell us that the baby had suddenly and for some unknown reason died in utero. Upon hearing the news, I became as numb and sick as in the days immediately after Kelsey's death.

Sam and Annie called later from the hospital. "This just can't be happening," Annie said in tears. When she told me the baby's name, Avery Parker Rennebohm, some of my sorrow lifted. I felt as though I knew him. They named him Avery because they liked the name, and Parker because it's the middle name of his maternal grandfather. I went outside in search of lilacs, gathered a few stems as well as some buttercups, and put them into a vase in front of the fireplace. Then, I lit a candle, and placed it next to the flowers, alongside a note Craig had written: "Avery Parker Rennebohm. We love you."

We tried to hold Sam and Annie in their sorrow, to share with them some of what we had learned over eight years of grieving, but every loss is different. Sam and Annie loved Avery from the moment they learned of his existence and will be forever affected by his death. But I'm sure they also will be touched by his presence. I have a framed quotation by an anonymous author on my kitchen windowsill:

> *Those I have loved, though now beyond my view,*
> *have given form and quality to my being.*
> *They have led me into the wide universe*
> *I continue to inhabit, and their presence*
> *is more vital to me than their absence.*

When I was on an early morning beach walk not long after Avery died, I sat for a while on a long driftwood log, smelling the seaweed, feeling the mist on my face, watching as the rising sun created thousands of tiny diamonds chasing one another across Port Townsend Bay. When the sun rose high enough to warm my face, I took off my jean jacket and placed it near the end of the log. I noticed a large round hole, worn to a fine finish by years of tossing in the rising and falling tides, and bent to examine it. Nestled within the hole was a spider's web and within the web was a mass of shiny, mustard-colored eggs. A few teensy-weensy spiders climbed up and down the delicate threads of the web.

I was in a liminal state between this world and the next, my heart aching at the loss of Avery. It occurred to me that the web might contain a message, so I focused on it, barely blinking. Soon, a sizable section of the mass of eggs began to pulsate. I held my breath. The mass expanded and contracted again and again until it finally burst, releasing a host of yellow spiders, each smaller than a speck of dirt. The remaining much-smaller mass of eggs began another rhythmic pulsing until it also ruptured. My arms were covered in goosebumps. It seemed to me that the spider web and eggs were indeed giving me a message, and it was this: Because of Avery's death, something new would be born. Another child? Possibly. A new way of being for Sam and Annie? Almost certainly.

I don't know if you can be with Avery, Kelsey. I think you can in ways I don't understand. Can you comfort him, put your arms around him, care for him, love him? Tell him we are forever changed because of him?

Yes, Avery's with me—and we're with each of you.

Sam called me a few months after Avery's death, sobbing, grieving not only for Avery but also for Kelsey, in some ways more intensely than he had right after her death—raw, open in new ways to the mystery of life and death. Although I ached for him, I also trusted he would emerge from the pain stronger and more open than ever before to both sorrow and joy.

Sam and Annie's third baby, Lila Ann, was born just six days after the first anniversary of Avery's death. Her brother, Willie, even at three, knew about death. I think for him it meant *not here*, and he knew enough to worry about those he loves. "Are you going to die,

Bee?" he asked me one day.

"I am, Willie, but hopefully not for a long time."

He asked me this before he left for daycare on a morning when I was at his house, taking care of Lila. When he returned home that evening, I wasn't there—I'd gone home earlier—and he burst into tears. Sam talked with him, and then the two of them phoned me. "Willie, were you worried about something all day?" Sam coached.

"Yes."

"What were you worried about?"

"That Bee will die."

So hard, this mortality of ours! Such a hard thing to get our heads and hearts around. I trust that as he grows, Willie will learn that love is stronger than death. Lila, herself, is such a joyful creature—smiling, dancing, adoring of her big brother. Light and love asserting themselves over sadness, loss, and despair.

I'm sad at the loss of Avery, but at the same time I'm also aware of the joy that is Kelsey and Avery, the joy that is God that is Kelsey and Avery. And I'm a grandmother to two grandsons, one in this world and one in the world beyond—and now to two granddaughters. Max and Alexandra's daughter, Amaya Marie, was born three months after Lila. She is a delight, open to adventure with a wonderful sense of humor and ready laughter.

Soon after Avery's death, our small drumming circle met on the back deck of our Marrowstone home, overlooking flowering herbs and climbing roses. The dogwood tree, planted years ago by friends to honor Kelsey, was in abundant bloom with scores of white flowers edged with pink—and one, just one, entirely pink flower. Every year since Kelsey's death the tree has bloomed with a single all-pink flower amid a cacophony of white. Craig has always noticed, and always commented on it.

In my drumming journey, birdsong accompanied me as I flew to the ocean. Waves crashed over me, and suddenly Avery was present. A very wise soul. As we walked together on a meandering path through the forest, he told me that he is always watching over Sam, Annie, and Willie and holding them closely. I stayed with him for a while, feeling his warmth and wisdom flow into my heart. That I'm a grandmother to an old soul was startling, but then I realized: My journey through grief has never made literal sense; rather, it's been an attempt to move beyond thinking to a place of openness, connection, and love.

Whenever Kelsey returned home for a visit, we picked her up at the airport. She always walked toward us with a bag slung over a shoulder and a big grin on her face. If she were to visit now, so much would have changed. For starters, she'd be thirty-eight, not twenty-eight. She probably would be well established in a career as a family counselor or maybe a clinical psychologist like Sam. She might be married with a child or two. If the past ten years were just a dream and she were to walk through our front door, I'd put my arms around her, smell her scent, feel her hair against my cheek, listen to her breathing. I'd revel in her physical presence. I can almost taste the joy of that homecoming, but then my heart seizes when I realize for probably the millionth time that I won't be able to hold her in my arms ever again.

But although she's not physically here, in some ways she's more accessible to me than if she were alive. Yesterday, I heard someone speaking in Spanish on my car radio, and suddenly I was remembering Kelsey's fluency in Spanish and thinking about how much good she could be doing in the world if only she had lived. My heart constricted in pain, and I felt tears forming behind my eyes.

Oh Kelsey, this is still hard. I still miss you so damned much.
Then I listened for her words.

I know, Mom, but I'm still here. We're on a journey together. Always. Forever.

Acknowledgments

The process of writing this memoir has paralleled my grieving, and I have never been alone on either journey. I am forever grateful to all those who have accompanied me. Pam Grossman walked with me from the very beginning, providing poetry, books, a steady stream of texts, and regular conversation. Hours spent with her and her husband, David Kahn, at their home and ours, on drives to Half Moon Bay, and in restaurants on both coasts were immensely healing. Kristi Rennebohm Franz and Eldon Franz were with us on the day we learned of Kelsey's death, and Eldon made critical arrangements to help us get to Boston and back. They seemed to know throughout the next weeks and months exactly when we most needed a shoulder to cry on. Jim, Lindsay, Charlie, and Melissa Bennett drove for hours to be with us on that awful day as did Laurie and John Danahy. Also with us were Benj Franz, Betty and Bill Rennebohm, Eleanor Bennett, Tom Dyer, Lise Kenworthy, Tricia and Steve Trainer, Sarah Trainer, Christina Leber, Annie Gayman, and Ben and Rachel Grossman-Kahn. Holly Miller and Pam Grossman provided food when doing so was important but the last thing on our minds. Camy Barrantes was with us during our first morning in Boston. Diane and Ray Hazen drove us around Kelsey's neighborhood. Kelsey's Boston friends—Ginny Blair Lougee, Jack Barrett, Ada Gunning, Molly Kocher, Shelley Wickham and students from the Boston College Mental Health Counseling Program—gave us, in addition to support, the gift of laughter. Boston College and Father MacMillan, in particular, offered us sacred space. Kelsey's New York City friends—Katie Broitman, Ruby Sheets, Bruce Sheets, Louise Sheets, Naima Coster, Xiomara Maldonado, Natalie Bell, Shira Backer, Perry Briskin, Bin Jung, Kenny Luguya, and many others—extended their love for Kelsey by becoming our friends. Liz Sims, Bonnie Morita, and Jim Paulson helped us sort through the boxes of Kelsey's belongings and have supported us in countless ways over the years.

Rachel Smith validated my feelings, even those I wasn't proud of. Kira Franz-Knight baked a cake for Max, making sure his birthday wasn't forgotten. Steve Clagett recorded Kelsey's voice mail greeting and videotaped the memorial service. Sarah Grossman-Kahn sang the Debbie Friedman songs that so sustained us. Amy Broitman sent me a novel, the first book other than poetry I was able to read, and Peter Broitman gave us the gift of stories. David Kahn named a star for Kelsey. Lenore Rubin sparked my interest in shamanic healing. Patty Cannon accompanied me on long walks. Lesley Burvill Holmes and Judith Gille held me when I could barely get through the days. Kathleen Brooker drove me to my book club when doing so was beyond my ability. The members of my book club— Kathleen Brooker, Susan Monas, Francie Ringold, Betsy Chamberlin, Laurel Clark, Anya LevySmith, Gabrielle O'Malley, and Liz Sims—shared, in one unforgettable night, their own experiences of grief. My WEB reading group members—Sue Morgan, Pam Forgey, Mary Traverse, Diane Hazen, Kristi Rennebohm Franz, Jane Braziunas, and Ginny Conrow—gave encouragement through books, great food, and laughter. Gillian and Michael Hund, traveled from Australia to be present for Kelsey's memorial service and were among those, including Ginny Blair Thompson, Beth Meister, Claire Hendrickson, and Kelsey's New York City friends, who planted magnolia trees in honor of Kelsey. Tom Hamilton, Jean Theroux, and Scott Simpson sent supportive texts, emails, cards, and art. Joanie and Bob Fisher opened their hearts and home to our family. Ann Hamilton O'Reilly, Amy Paz, and Rob Paz were present when we needed them. Martha Lawson, Liziah Richards, Gail Connelly and other staff from Seattle Public Schools gave plants, understanding, and friendship. Beth Meister reminded me that Kelsey was "home" and then became part of my emotional home. Charlie Bennett reminded me that Kelsey "always understood". Delcy Marulanda gave us a clean apartment to return home to when it meant the most. Kathy Williams was the first bereaved mom I spoke with— and gave me my first grief book. Bob Dell and the "Pathways to Promise" staff sent wind chimes to remind us of Kelsey. The entire Sarju family—Dave, Michelle, Ziah, Zeke, and Nyasha—accompanied us at various times along the journey. Kelsey's Boston College mentor and major professor, Brinton Lykes, spearheaded a scholarship in Kelsey's honor, kept us apprised of the recipients, and stayed in touch. Erin Rennebohm, joined with me in acknowledging the importance of stones. Gary Karp pointed out the hopefulness of rainbows. Michaela Karp deepened my belief in intuition. Robin Gaphni was an amazingly supportive—and surprisingly fun—companion in grief. Nancy Kreuger and then Diana Burnett and Kayley Groundwater allowed me to become their companion. Corby Fleming regularly sent me photos of her "Kelsey" garden. John Bennett spoke Kelsey's name every time we talked. Deni Deutsch Marshall and I had regular conversations about grief and Judaism, including a very special weekend at Point Reyes. Arthor Dorros spent the first Christmas Eve after Kelsey's death with us, our conversation transforming sorrow into meaning. Alex Dorros gave us delicious food and stories. Beth Huppin was not only a gifted teacher but asked questions and gently pushed me in new directions. Julie and Theo Wierdsma buoyed us through laughter, long walks above beautiful beaches, glasses of wine while watching Hawaiian sunsets, and delicious meals. Jennifer Parker and Linda Secord knitted me scarves, knotting in love with each stitch. With Linda and Mark Secord, we drummed our way to a better place. Scott Simpson and Alyssa Stepan-Simpson sent us an Amish heart quilt and remembered Kelsey in so many thoughtful ways. Kelsey's childhood friends– Whitney Johnson, Summer Haskell, Jessie and Arielle Paulson, Rachel Smith, Erin Counts, Ben and Becky Grossman-Kahn, Clover Muters McIngalls, and Betsy Conrad Edholm—sent photos and shared memories. My childhood friends—Barbara King, Kristen Dyson, Cheryl Nimz, Julie Casagrande, Adrianne Casey, Nancy Prickett, Barbara Cheney, Rita Conrad, and Ann Massing—nurtured me through emails and texts and especially during our reunions. Michael, Molly, and Sarah Danahy, Katie Broitman, Ben McKay, Nathan Bennett, Kassia Bennett, Ziah Sarju, Tom Dyer, Sallie Reynolds, Kathleen Brooker, Tim McDaniel, Steve Clagett, Jennifer Parker, Deni Deutsch Marshall, Steve Marshall, Jane Fellner, Neal Friedman, Betsy Hanson, Richard Pulkrabek, Lesley Burvill Holmes, Judith Gille, Tom Butts, Diane Hazen, Ray Hazen, Kristi Rennebohm Franz, Eldon Franz, Ruby Sheets, Louise Sheets, Way of the Spirit retreatants, Pathways to Promise staff, and many others brought their love and laughter on overnight visits to our Marrowstone home.

The members of Plymouth, Prospect and Pilgrim churches supported us through Kelsey's memorial service and beyond. Port Townsend
Friends Meeting, especially Sandy Harold, Cathy Thomas, Carla
Main, Hannah Russell, Shirley McRae, Heather Woolf McRae, Jef-
frey Clark, Orlanda McRae Clark, Monica Fletcher, Steve Evans,
Tom Butts, Katy Festinger, Laura Martin, Michael Buettner, Nyla
Dartt, and Deborah Lewis listened to us in the silence, and held us
close. Rob Rennebohm often showed up at our house to provide
wise doctoring and gentle humor. Ken and Beth Kraybill encouraged me to share my experience of trauma and healing with others.
Members of my spiritual nurture group, Cathy Thomas, Carla Main,
and Deborah Lewis loved me unconditionally. My Way of the Spirit
sisters—Carmela Alexander, Jeanne Bourget, Susanne Ratcliffe
Wilson, Anne Mills, Nancy Mellor, and Jade Rockwell Crown—
changed my life. My spiritual teachers, Jane Fleming, Christine
Hall, Elaine Emily, and Cathy Walling validated the "voice within"
and provided care and guidance. Nazire Argeso, Nurten Ozmelek,
Selda Argeso Turkman, and Nilgun Argeso, along with their children and husbands became my family.   With Annie Mize, I often
walked a labyrinth on Marrowstone Island which had been constructed by Jane Fleming, Toni Harris, and Amanda Sargent. I hold
dear all our nieces and nephews: Brynn Orechia, Melissa Bennett,
Charlie Bennett, Luke Bennett, Nathan Bennett, Heather Fisher,
Erin Rennebohm, Annie Veit, Michael Danahy, Molly Danahy,
Wendy Torrence, Benj Franz, and Zac Franz. Thank you, thank you,
thank you to all who cared for us over the years, all those I've named
and so many more. Your encouragement, love, and care made all the
difference.

Over the past decade, I've had several wonderful writing instructors
including Anna Quinn, Kathryn Hunt, Sayantani Dasgupta, Sheila
Bender, and Emily Rapp Black. The first person to give me advice
on my manuscript was Barbara Sjoholm who took me aback (rightly
so) by kindly pointing out all that I'd left out. Emily Rapp Black
asked important questions, the responses to which doubled my manuscript. Robin Cruise provided astute editing, taught me to pay attention, and made the book so much better than it would have been
otherwise. The members of my writing group—Pam Sampel, Jenni-

fer Goff, Kelly Anderson, and Linda Secord—provided years of retreats and inspired me through their comments and their own writing. The words of Esther Levy, Becky Benson, and Emily Rapp Black of the Loss Ladies writing group were spot on. Pam Grossman, Cathy Thomas, and Suzanne Pitre read multiple drafts or reread the same draft multiple times, going far beyond the call of friendship. Celeste Dybeck, an elder of the Jamestown S'Klallam tribe and Rabbi Deni Marshall read pertinent sections of the book for accuracy and to look for instances of cultural appropriation. Ruthi and Mike Winter and Betsy Borrow Stern were great cheerleaders and inspired me through their art, music, and words. Betsy Hanson prodded me to find a way to get this book to a wider audience—and Jodie Toohey of Legacy Book Press offered a way to do it. Kira Franz-Knight captured the essence of the book with a few artistic strokes—and Kaitlea Toohey provided the finishing touches. Thank you to all of you for giving me hours of pleasure and helping me share my story.

The love, laughter, and support of Sam Rennebohm, Annie Gayman, Max and Alexandra Ndegwa Rennebohm, Willie and Lila Rennebohm, and Amaya Ndegwa Rennebohm have enriched my life beyond measure. My gratitude to you is enormous and my love unending. Craig has been my soul mate, steady companion in good times and bad, constant source of comfort, valued advisor, and greatest cheerleader. Words alone can't express how much I love you, how thankful I am to share this life with you.

About the Author

After a long career in education—teacher, school psychologist, administrator, and consultant—Barbara retired (with her husband) to a very small island in the Salish Sea, where she taught occasional workshops on the impact of emotional trauma and spent time gardening, walking on the beach, writing, drumming, visiting friends, and taking part in her Quaker Meeting. She and her husband moved from their island home back to Seattle in order to be closer to their sons, daughters-in-law, and three young grandchildren. Kelsey, who died in 2012, is an ever-present part of their lives. Two essays adapted from her memoir have been published in The Friends Journal and What Canst Thou Say. Another essay based on her work with children and families experiencing homelessness was published in *The New Educator*.

www.ingramcontent.com/pod-product-compliance
Lightning Source LLC
Chambersburg PA
CBHW020416150626
46554CB00014B/1728